MURPHY'S LORE

BOB MURPHY

MURPHY'S LORE
TALES FROM THE WEST

NERO

Published by Nero.,
an imprint of Schwartz Publishing Pty Ltd
37–39 Langridge Street
Collingwood VIC 3066 Australia
email: enquiries@blackincbooks.com
www.nerobooks.com.au

The National Library of Australia Cataloguing-in-Publication entry:

Murphy, Bob, 1982–
Murphy's lore: tales from the west / Bob Murphy.
9781863957281 (paperback)
9781925203240 (ebook)
Murphy, Bob, 1982–
Western Bulldogs (Football team). Australian football players—Anecdotes.
Australian football—Anecdotes. Australian newspapers—Sections, columns, etc.—Sports.
Sports journalism.
796.336092

Book design by Peter Long

This book is dedicated to Arthur:
the body of a sausage with the heart of a bulldog.

CONTENTS

2009

2010

2014

INTRODUCTION

When I started penning columns for *The Age* in 2007, I wanted to write about all the things I loved about footy. Funnily enough, at the time I was feeling a little disillusioned with the game and my place in it.

I was 24 years old, about to become a father for the first time, and I had recently wrecked my knee in spectacular fashion. Changes on such a big scale were leading me to ponder the bigger questions in life. I think the columns I wrote, particularly the early ones, were a reaction to this. With hindsight, I can see I was counselling myself, reminding myself of all the beautiful things about a footballer's lot.

Over time, the column became like a good friend I could confide in. Sometimes, writing it was a cathartic exercise for me, helping me to make sense of the madness on the field; at other times it let me step back and smell the roses for a bit. But more often than not it was simply a chance for me to look at the game from a different angle and have some fun with it.

The very first column in this compendium is more or less the first thing I had written since I left school. Its themes of tribe, family, anticipation, nostalgia and moving from one place to another are ones that I came back to again and again.

There was always a considered recklessness when it came to writing my weekly column. I tried to embrace the Pro Hart philosophy of putting all the ideas down on the page and then making something of it. I was learning as I went, and every misstep, every wrong turn was on display in Thursday's paper. In that regard, my writing and footy skills are very similar! As they say, you've got to crack a few eggs to make an omelette. When I felt I had got it right, though, when I was able to capture exactly what I wanted with the right words, the sense of exhilaration was the same as in the best moments I have ever had on a football field.

The 2012 piece I wrote about what it was like to play on Steve Johnson was a turning point. The response to that column showed me that there is no substitute for taking the reader out onto the field of play. I think it's the best thing I've ever written, and it was also one of the easiest to write. I remember waking up the morning after the game and scrawling down on some paper the things Stevie had said to me. His quotes became the bones and flesh of that piece; all I had to do was shade in the face.

Taking up a role in the media while I was still playing had an element of risk. I was barely into the middle of my footy career when I started at *The Age*, and still establishing myself. I was certainly not a household name, unlike other player columnists. After years of virtual anonymity, suddenly I was more visible. Early on, I remember a woman sidling up to me in a

Carlton bookstore and whispering in my ear, 'You're not as interesting as you think you are,' which was unsettling, to say the least!

I often wondered whether my club and my coaches were totally comfortable with me having a weekly column while I was still developing as a player. My aim right from the start was to give people an insight into a player's world, while doing my best to avoid embarrassing my teammates or my club. If my coaches did have any concerns, I'm thankful that they trusted me and left me to it.

Something that did surprise me was how varied the reactions from opposition players were. In the very first year of the column, I remember a seething Fraser Gehrig, under lights at Etihad Stadium, spitting out, 'How the hell are you writing for a newspaper?' In later years, by contrast, Geelong's Harry Taylor shook my hand at the end of a game and told me how much he enjoyed reading the column every week. To think of players at other clubs reading my weekly ramblings still seems very strange to me, but I'm told that some did.

I think writing about footy made me a better footballer. Life can move pretty fast for your average player, and the ritual of sitting down each week to sketch out a story gave me some perspective. It allowed me to slow down for a bit and really think hard about what was happening around me. It also gave me the space to create something, and so became a way for me to build some self-esteem that sat parallel to kicks and hand-balls, wins and losses. Writing gave me balance.

Looking back over every column for this project has been, as you might expect, an unusual experience. Mercifully, it was far more enjoyable than I'd anticipated. If I had to pick a favourite, I think it would be the piece I wrote about a day I spent at the MCG watching Carlton and Richmond with my son, Jarvis, who proudly wore his Bulldogs jumper for the whole day. At the time, that column felt like a bit of a throwaway, but reading it now makes me thankful I took up writing in the first place. I'm sure it'll feel even more special as the years go by and my little ones grow up.

I might have been feeling a little lost when I began my weekly column back in 2007, but with each passing season that feeling faded away. As the years rolled by, I was left with an overwhelming sense of wonder and gratitude. Grateful to still be out there living my childhood dream, and grateful for a loving family (including Arthur, of course), for a proud and loyal football club, and for a great game that keeps sweeping me off my feet after all these years.

January 2015

2007

HERE COME FOOTY'S TRIBES

I woke on Monday to walk the dog around my neighbourhood, as I do most mornings, and three things dawned on me. The first was the sun, which doesn't count. The second was the bitter cold, which made me realise winter was almost upon us. The excitement I felt is usually reserved for young children on Christmas morning.

The third thing that stopped me short was walking by the old football ground on Brunswick Street, the home of that ancient tribe known as Fitzroy. It was a sobering moment, as we all know that this tribe was lost several years ago to the harsh realities of the national competition.

It's usually about this time of year that some well-worn football terminology is wheeled out and given a spit and shine for the new season. My personal favourite, and one I'm sure you're all familiar with, is 'football is tribal'.

Tribal warfare, of course, dates back to the very core of civilisation on almost every continent on Earth. It's an easy connection to make, what with the colours, home territory, team hierarchy and the fact that every weekend for the next 26 weeks, various teams in their tribal colours will take to the field to try to beat the others into submission. Team colours and mascots are something all genuine club supporters hold dear, and the notion that you 'bleed for the jumper' is something that still rings true for all clubs.

The notion of football being tribal warfare might be a bit too Hollywood or a touch romantic for some, but I believe it is a very endearing aspect of our game, something that has been bruised over the past few weeks.

Of Australia's major cities, Melbourne, in particular, is sports-crazed – and I hope it always will be. You can really feel that, over summer, people have been building up to this weekend – Round One.

The very nature of being a part of a tribe is that you're passionate about the cause. I couldn't begin to count the number of people in the street who have been asking me how our tribe, the Bulldogs, will fare this year.

It is not just some colours that contribute to tribalism. My research tells me that within the tribes will be a smaller, close-knit group of warriors who will go to the front line to fight for their pride and territory. These are the 22 players who will run out this weekend.

In this group there will be warriors old and new. The elders will have memories of glorious September victories, of standing aloft before their weary and beaten opponents, and they will have the scars to show for their troubles. The young men will bristle with nerves and excitement, and revel in wearing the colours for the first time. All share a sense of purpose.

The national competition brings with it a combination of tribes near and far, some with rich histories of September triumph and others with dreams and not so much in the vaults. Each of the 16 tribes about to do battle has been carefully planning for many, many months. I would even suggest that every single one of them would have been meticulously planning this weekend straight after the West Coast Eagles held the holy grail high for all to see on 30 September last year.

After such a long and eventful layoff, you can almost sense a feeling of relief from all levels of the game – from the AFL Commission and the club supporters all the way down to lowly footballers-turned-columnists. It all starts again tomorrow night, and you can bet that all the tribes are on notice and ready for a fight.

Ladies and gentleman, take your seats. Round One – ding, ding!

29 March 2007

WINNING AND LOSING GETS SERIOUS

When I was a wee lad growing up, it seemed that – apart from sleeping and eating – all I was ever doing was competing in some sort of sporting event, be it football, tennis or cricket. All my memories from this time are ones I cherish; they have a real *Wonder Years* feel to them.

These blissful childhood memories have failed to acknowledge losing – at least, the pain of losing, anyway. I know I suffered some defeats in junior sport . . . didn't I?

I certainly recall a heavy 10–0 defeat in only my second appearance for Warragul United Soccer Club. It was to be my last appearance in the shinguards, although I don't think I stopped playing due to the pain of defeat. In fact, as I recall, my teammates and I slid down the muddy banks of the soccer ground on our bellies at game's end, apparently oblivious to the fact the opposing team were enjoying the spoils of victory.

Fast-forward 12 years, and defeat brings with it a whole new feel. Gone are the mudslides (rightly or wrongly) and in their place are team meetings, sleepless nights, anxiety and in-depth analysis. In this age of professional sport, when you put so much time, effort and passion into one thing and fall well short on the big stage, deflation will always follow.

My team's loss on the weekend was quite severe, and the feeling in the rooms afterwards was closer to that of a funeral than a football game. The post-match address from our coach just confirmed our poor showing, and as my team-mates and I trudged towards our cars to go home, we knew there was a bit more pain to endure before the next week-end's game.

Monday morning starts with an ocean swim at Port Melbourne to get rid of the sore spots. It's funny how, after a loss, the water seems to drop a few degrees, and how your Speedos seem minuscule as you go to put them on in front of the TV crews huddled on the beach.

The team review meeting scheduled for later that morning looms as a possible triple root canal. The meeting is spirited and home truths fly. It is a necessary evil, and while it is a tense half-hour, you can feel the mood of the whole club lift. By the time we leave the meeting room we all have a bounce back in our step.

The next day also begins with a dip in the sea, this time at Williamstown. The water, while still freezing, seems to have warmed a degree or two. Some players believe this to be due to a geographical change from one beach to another. Others believe the water is warmer not only because the review meeting is over, but also because it was positive; their bodies have responded accordingly. Or it could be global warming. It's hard to know.

After pacing up and down the beach, a few of us dive under and the ice hits our lungs. It's invigorating. It almost feels as though we are washing away our sins from the weekend's game. It was Easter, after all, and it seems we have now risen.

Thankfully, after a pretty miserable couple of days the sun has come up, and we can finally move on to more pressing matters. The coaching staff are in full swing for our next opponent. Theories and tactics are given to players to pore over. This got me thinking about the tactics and strategies I was receiving 12 years ago.

Most young boys starting out in the game will be heavily influenced by their fathers, who advise them much like coaches do. Obviously, Rodney Eade's instructions are somewhat more sophisticated than what Dad was passing on to me, but you get the picture.

I loved junior football. I loved the unpredictability of the game even then. My home town, Warragul, is surrounded by a dozen or so smaller towns, all surrounded by rolling green hills. And so on Saturday mornings there was always a short drive to the game.

I'd ride up the front with my dad. My knees would bounce with excitement for the whole trip. Every week he'd have the same advice: kick with both feet and hold on to your chest marks.

Sound advice. I think Dad must have known not to overburden me with too much theory. My school reports alone would have helped him make that judgement.

The game has changed so much, and losing has taken on a whole new face. But as I drive to the game by myself this week I'll still hear my dad's words in my head: kick with both feet and hold on to your chest marks.

Will do, Dad. Thanks, mate.

12 April 2007

I almost got it right, but I left out the
third part of Dad's holy trinity of footy wisdom.
1. Kick with both feet.
2. Hold on to your chest marks.
3. Find a man.

IMAGINE, A SIDE WITH RHYTHM

For as long as there has been music, there have been rock stars.
Even back to the days of classical composers such as Beethoven,
and right through to the age of rock 'n' roll when Elvis and the
Beatles took centre stage, musicians have been the obsession of
popular culture.

As the popular music of the day has changed, so of course
have the rock stars themselves and their flamboyant lifestyles.
It seems that rock stars represent a life of fantasy. In an age
where fantasy football teams dominate the internet, I thought
I would do my own. Not a fantasy football team made up of
modern footballers, but a team of genuine rock stars.

As the chairman of selectors, it is my pleasure to go through
the starting line-up for Round One – my team for the Fantasy
Football League (or the FFL, as it is known). It is worth noting
that the senior coach for 2007 will be Ozzy Osbourne. Ozzy,
team physiotherapist Elton John and I make up the match
committee. Let's start with the back six . . .

BACKS

Johnny Cash: A reliable back pocket, slow and steady, with a particular dislike for establishment figures. At his personal request, the team uniform is completely black. Jumper, shorts, socks and boots.

Jimi Hendrix: One of the most naturally gifted full backs in memory. His left foot is deadly at kick-outs, and his colourful headbands are a hit with his young fans. Unstoppable when he's on fire.

Nick Cave: The lanky Australian will play on the opposition's resting ruckman. Has come under criticism for his negative outlook on the team, himself, his coach and just about everything else life has to offer.

HALF-BACKS

Janis Joplin: Widely regarded as the toughest player on the team, she will tag the opposition's best forward and do whatever it takes to put them off their game.

Kurt Cobain: A standout loner in a team that is full of them. His moods can swing as wildly as his kicking boot. At the heart of team spirit.

Paul Kelly: The experienced defender had a mixed pre-season but his training form of late has come on in leaps and bounds. We have relied on this home-grown talent to produce the goods year after year, making him one of the first to get a gig.

I asked Coach Osbourne for his comment on the back six, and all he said was, 'I don't know who you are and I've never heard of Paul Kelly... here, talk to Sharon.'

CENTRE

Mick Jagger: The lightly built veteran just keeps performing. His heroics in big games many years ago cannot be denied. Nor can the fact he has tried to sleep with most of his teammates' wives.

John Lennon: The volatile superstar recruited from Liverpool has taken all before him. Imagine all the people if he wasn't playing, a sad thought. Insisted Yoko come to all team meetings and football trips, alienating some teammates.

Keith Richards: The other half of the Glimmer Twins across the centre line. The durability of this man is astounding. He has racked up 457 games consecutively, which is particularly remarkable considering his colourful post-game habits. Seems to produce some of his best when on tour. Amazingly, looks to have a few good years left in him.

Ozzy had this to say: 'What is Australian rules? Is this a prank?'

HALF-FORWARDS

Tim Rogers: Has all the moves and the spirit to be anything, however he still goes under the radar with a lot of supporters.

Tex Perkins: A real glamour boy, and the coach loves his physical presence. It seems the girls who wait by his car after training are also mindful of his physical presence.

Bon Scott: Completes what is a mercurial half-forward line. His no-frills approach and willingness to do the dirty deeds make him a favourite with all the working-class fans. Nicknamed 'TNT' because he can blow a game apart. Believed to be fending off interest from Fremantle.

FORWARDS

Gallagher, N: There is no doubt about this boy's ability. It's just whether or not he can stop arguing with his brother long enough to show us his God-given talents. He could do without the cigarettes and alcohol.

Elvis Presley (c): We know him, of course, as 'the King'. The team captain's heroics are that of legend. His appetite is also legendary and has recently prompted some supporters to dub him the 'the Burger King'. Has had more comebacks than Sinatra, but his skinfolds now appear to have snuffed out a glorious farewell that would be fitting for our greatest champion.

Gallagher, L: In a team full of cockiness and bravado, this young man stands head and shoulders above the rest in that department. He would have been left in the reserves for his arrogance if he were not such an out-and-out star.

Ozzy had this pearl of wisdom to describe his flashy forwards: 'Who is Tex Rogers?'

FOLLOWERS

Paul McCartney: Don't let his lack of height fool you. He seems to have wings attached and is a creative genius in the ruck, with amazing reach. Another of the team's left-footers; whoever he plays for invariably seems to spend a bit of time at number one.

George Harrison: Quiet achiever who goes about his business without much fanfare, but highly respected by his teammates. Bit of a dark horse.

Ringo Starr: This pocket dynamo is not the most talented in the group but always has his nose over the ball and lightens the mood with one-liners. Our 'Fab Four' is the envy of the competition.

INTERCHANGE

Pete Doherty: Coming back from suspension for a series of misdemeanours; has been given a second chance mainly because he agreed to bring Kate Moss to all home games.

Axl Rose: Normally a walk-up start for the XVIII but his failure to show up for last week's practice match saw him sanctioned by the team's leadership group.

Bob Dylan: An inspiration to the younger boys in our team, and one of the most influential and creative players we've seen. He is adaptable to most conditions, even if the wind blows or times change. Handy when played left of centre.

Jimmy Page: In case we want a burst of genuine pace or some grunt off the bench.

It promises to be one hell of a season, full of all the thrills and spills you've come to expect. This Saturday's home game at Strawberry Fields (SF) will be live into Melbourne, so check your local guides.

17 May 2007

OF BUTTERFLIES AND BULLDOGS

If you are someone who looks for beauty in obscure places, then I'm sure you'll be familiar with the life cycle of the butterfly, the genesis of which is the caterpillar, hardly the most glamorous species in the animal kingdom.

What the caterpillar lacks in physical beauty it more than makes up for with patience, quietly putting together a cocoon in which it undergoes a stunning metamorphosis, and emerging to show the world its breathtaking arsenal of colour and acrobatics. From there, the butterfly leads a life full of excitement and thrills, all the while using the world as its stage and the rest of us, looking on in wonder, as its audience.

Sadly, this life is one that is short-lived. The butterfly lives its life to the full, but I can't help wondering if it knows its demise is never too far away. The life cycle of a butterfly is not too dissimilar to that of an elite athlete. Athletes at the top of their sport are on 'borrowed time', and it is something that plays on all of their minds at some point.

The average career of an AFL footballer is about 43 games – not even two seasons. Whenever footballers are interviewed, especially when they are just starting out, you hear them hope – or, better, 'wish' – for a career in the vicinity of ten years. To a play at the highest level for a decade is a great achievement; to do it at one club is herculean.

Ten years sounds like a lot more than a butterfly's lifetime of a couple of weeks, but we are bigger than them, so on my Duckworth-Lewis system it's an even match.

It takes a long time to get to the physical and mental state to be given a chance to play elite level sport; just like the butterfly, some careful planning has gone in well before you emerge from your cocoon to take the field in game number one.

My memories of my first year at the Bulldogs in 2000 are quite vague: I'd just turned 18 and was struggling to finish off my schooling. I don't mind saying I was a little vague myself. But one clear memory I have is of listening to then captain Scott Wynd as he stood in front of the players and announced his retirement.

To see such a big man fighting back tears created an atmosphere that was wonderful and tragic in the same moment. It hit home to me then how much this game meant to those men in the room. I could not begin to imagine what the older players were feeling as their leader told them he could go no further.

Since that time, there has been a small but steady flow of players retire in similar circumstances, and each time the gravity of the situation hits home more heavily. I suppose a lot of that has to do with knowing that I am one year closer to a similar fate.

When a long-serving player retires, the public gets to see the news conference and the final game. The player being chaired off by his comrades is often the lasting impression he leaves the game with, but for me, the footballer's equivalent of a funeral is that announcement to the playing group – only at this funeral, you have to give your own eulogy.

Like any such occasion, it forces you to look at your own mortality, whether you want to or not. It is another look at how wonderful this game is, though. I like to think that this game is about young, fiercely driven men giving their best years to their chosen trade.

To describe the best athletes in our game, I would use the analogy of a boy soprano whose voice is so perfect it sounds almost otherworldly. Their talent burns so very bright but awfully brief. Thankfully for us, castration was never entertained as a viable option to prolong our careers, just as the boy soprano endured all those years ago.

Back to that meeting in 2000. When the great Wynd flicked the bails, I was sat with six other first-year players and a few guys in their second seasons. All of us were spellbound, and I think I can safely assume all of us were contemplating what our careers would hold for us.

Out of this small group, some would go on to forge terrific careers. Daniel Giansiracusa, Lindsay Gilbee, Ryan Hargrave, Mitch Hahn and I have been lucky enough to play 100 games. But what about the others? Patrick Bowden was a casualty of trade week and landed at the Tigers, while Patrick Wiggins, Jay Solomon and Ricky Symes all had their football dreams crushed by the cut-throat nature of the competition.

For those of us fortunate to still be running around, it is a great motivation to push on. I think it was Neil Young who said 'it's better to burn out than to fade away'. That really encapsulates my point: football is an all-too brief career.

Thankfully, that day is far off in the distance, and there is still plenty of time to shine as brightly as those butterflies, or soar to the heights of the boy sopranos.

24 May 2007

FLYING SQUAD IN PLANE CLOTHES

'On the road again . . . I just can't wait to get on the road again . . .' Country music icon Willie Nelson put it so simply and so brilliantly in his signature tune. Interstate dominance is a hot topic on the AFL agenda these days, so much so that an investigation is underway into why those clubs have had so much recent success.

My boys, the Bulldogs, are one week into a two-week road trip, and I'm guessing that a lot of football followers are intrigued by what goes on on tour. Just as I would wonder what Willie gets up to.

Travelling interstate with a footy team is not unlike a touring rock band. At least, that's what I think when we travel . . . it seems to lift my spirits and dispel homesickness. I understand it's a bit of a stretch, but with the trust we've built up in this column this year, I ask for leniency.

We assemble at the airport in our uniforms. As the Bulldogs prepared to fly to Brisbane last week, I noticed the rock group Dallas Crane was also checking in just down from us. They were dressed as you would want them to be: tight black jeans, country and western shirts, sunglasses that swallowed the features of their faces. 'Effortlessly cool' pretty much summed them up.

My teammates and I were also dressed as you would imagine: bright-blue parachute-material tracksuits. Not the most flattering of threads, and slightly less retro-cool, but it does boast our colours and logo, which mean the world to us.

It's funny how things in our universe are connected. Just as I was tucking in to my aeroplane snack of gourmet delights, I read that the Dalai Lama was in town to preach his philosophies on spirituality, happiness and, above all else, the ability to forgive your fellow man or woman.

Indeed, just as the Dalai travels the world preaching his message to a throng of followers, the 16 teams of the AFL travel the land preaching and selling their game style. I believe the message of my beloved Bulldogs is not unlike that of the Dalai Lama – we play with a passion unbridled, but we also play an unorthodox style of game that goes against the grain of the mainstream.

People generally will be a little frightened of something different. Our style of fast-running midgets and an even smaller forward line is often criticised, because in essence it hasn't been the done thing in this sport for the past 100 years. I like to think that we are the indie heroes of the competition – much like English rock band Arctic Monkeys – and we are daring to change the foundations of the game.

As we checked into our Brisbane hotel, it was down to business. The schedule is rigid and monitored to the letter.

Powerade is the drink of choice, and times are allocated for physiotherapy and massage.

Travel entails having a roommate, and it has taken me many years to find my interstate soulmate. Years of searching led me to Daniel Giansiracusa, a sweet young man with a heart the size of his head. As far as roommates go, I think we complement each other perfectly. We are as I imagine an old married couple in their 70s would be: the cups of tea flow, and there is never an argument over which movie to watch.

Pondering what was happening at Dallas Crane's hotel, I concluded that Powerade and physio would not have been on the menu, in their place a diet of beer, whisky and late-night jam sessions. Whatever serves the individual best, you could say.

For a third year running we managed to sneak away from Brisbane with the four points. Our brave and loyal supporters who made the trip north, and those sitting in their living rooms, were witness to a team taking to one knee with head bowed, begging forgiveness for recent wrongdoings.

Interstate wins are crucial tests in such a long year; they are not easy to come by. Team sport is an unequalled atmosphere of togetherness, and standing out on the Gabba pitch arm in arm at game's end was just reward for the hard yards of preparation, and crucially important for the fabric of a club that has so many young men new to the caper.

The experience of winning away from home knits a group closer and gets those in their first season or so to buy in to the cause even more. As we sang the cherished theme song, I again pondered the Melbourne rockers and how they would celebrate a successful gig. One suspects stretching down might not have

featured so much as staying up into the wee hours with someone like Tex Perkins, swapping stories of old tours and classic
gigs with a drink in hand.

We flew back from Brisvegas with a feeling of humility
and satisfaction. Waiting at the baggage claim was that other
band of tourists, Dallas Crane, seemingly nursing severe hangovers and with their elegantly wasted look down pat. Theirs
must have been a successful tour, too. Our boys, who were not
nursing hangovers as much as sore knees and ankles, also had
the look down pat – elegantly injured.

A few days of recovery and it's another road trip, this time
to Darwin. Our road crew will be working feverishly to get
things going for our gig against the Dockers. I imagine the
game will be sold out. It should be a rockin' night.

14 June 2007

CLUB SERVANTS STILL THE LIFEBLOOD OF THE BULLDOGS

The Bulldogs as a football club is virtually unrecognisable now compared with when I first walked through the door eight years ago. Coaches, players and facilities have all changed or been facelifted. Nathan Brown has gone – and also been facelifted, funnily enough. But despite all these changes to the facade, the heart of the west still beats true, thanks to the influence of passionate club servants.

Riding the emotional tidal waves of a season from inside the four walls of one of the 16 tribes can be exhausting, and may even bring on seasickness if you are not adequately prepared. Experience is a precious resource in the topsy-turvy circus I've come to call the home and away season.

What experience provides is the knowledge and ability to keep the ship of emotion steady on an ocean that can fluctuate from champagne football a fortnight ago to bottom-dweller the next. It can all change that quickly.

The most valuable people at every club are wise enough

not to get swept away by the dizzying euphoria of a big win, and not so foolish as to throw it all in after a couple of bad losses. Their effort and work ethic remains steady whether it rains, hails or shines.

At Footscray we are lucky enough to have a plethora of such people on call every day, servants of the club whose sole purpose is to help me and my boys get out there in the best possible condition each week.

It's almost become a cliche that the property steward and bootstudders are the lifeblood of an organisation that turns over millions of dollars a year. But for a working-class club like the Bulldogs, it is the volunteers who actually saved us a couple of times – the same volunteers who are still revered by all inside the four walls.

The changerooms at Telstra Dome are extremely cold, loud and bereft of atmosphere. Inside them, it is the faces of these people (in the latter stages of their middle-age) that light up the room with warm smiles and sincere words of good luck.

I would like to introduce the Good Samaritans of the Bull-dogs' support staff, starting with the match-day volunteers Ray Chalkey, Billy Wood, Ben Bradley, Lou Thompson and Alan Jackson. These men revel in all conditions and are responsible for security, boots, drink bottles and team morale.

They are the foot soldiers in an army run by two characters who throw a powerful shadow over the club: assistant property steward Noel Kinniburgh and his boss, Eddie Walsh. David Smorgon is the president and the face of the club, but I think even he would concede that these men hold a large stake of power at the Kennel.

Noel, who is the young up-and-comer and Eddie's

understudy, has been the Peter Costello of the Bulldogs party. Happy to serve the hierarchy the best way he can, while at the same time grooming himself for Eddie's (John Howard's, if you will) job. Noel's mantra is simple and successful: 'Get the job done.' He is a cult figure at the Kennel, and for the most part goes about his business with ease and little fuss.

But he also has a sharp sense of humour, which was on show one particular karaoke night when Noel sprang to life for his impromptu version of 'Rock Around the Clock'. The dancing was original and the acoustics unique, but he pulled it off and the boys showed their appreciation with a standing ovation.

Eddie is the all-knowing oracle of Footscray, a man who answers to no one. His reputation has been built on 60-odd years of impeccable service. Now in his 80s, Ed is not as quick off the mark as he used to be but is still capable in a one-on-one contest. While Noel is more comfortable in the spotlight, Eddie is far more at ease behind the scenes.

Not one to hand out socks or towels too easily in his early years, Ed has mellowed. In my first few years at the club I would always try to get a reaction from Ed by giving him a hug or offering my hand way up high for a return high-five. He always turned the offer down; I got the impression he wasn't too impressed with the idea of high-fiving a young punk who'd been at the club for a minute.

After a few more years, in which Eddie and I built up more trust and respect for each other, I'd given up the high-five approach. That was until one day a year or so ago, when I found myself walking past Eddie on my way to the physio room, only to lose my balance in shock as Ed (ever so nonchalantly) offered his hand way up high. Naturally, I took him up on the offer, and Ed just kept on walking as if nothing had happened.

That's my lasting impression of the great Eddie Walsh. A little man with a heart bigger than the suburb he's lived in his whole life.

Of course, you can't write a story like this without leaving some deserving people out: trainers, medical staff and others who are just as integral to a club's push for success. I'd also like to acknowledge Ray Chalkey, one of Eddie's trained men who is down on his luck at the moment. The whole club wishes him good health and a speedy recovery.

These precious jewels ask for nothing in return except to be part of the action. If some day we are lucky enough to go all the way, I'm sure they will be the first down to the Footscray Town Hall to congratulate the players.

If we are not so lucky, they will still be there, offering a word of encouragement or a pat on the back, just as they have been this last fortnight, keeping the ship steady as the seas of the season have turned rough. They are as much a part of the team as anyone.

2 August 2007

FOUR WALLS SHADE
US AS WE GROW

A friend told me recently about a dog that ran away from its New South Wales home. Lost dogs are common, but this particular pooch was found weeks later – in Darwin.

I couldn't help but ponder not only how the dog had made such a journey, but also why it had run away in the first place. Further still, what does 'home' mean? How does your home affect the way you are?

Home for me has changed over the years. Different houses, housemates and locations have all affected my sense of home. In my opinion, home is an underrated phenomenon. It's a place of refuge from the outside world, to sit with your nearest and dearest, share a meal and the difficulties and the spoils of life.

My memories of my first home are a bit vague, as I was three and a half when we left it. But what I lack in recall is compensated by the warmth that can only come from having a loving family with whom to learn the tricks of the trade.

After my first steps in our humble home in Ballarat, we

packed up our little circus and moved to the green fields of Warragul. The house that Mum and Dad settled on was not the sort you would find on *MTV Cribs*, but it was ours.

More importantly, it had a huge gum tree that we named Herbie in the front yard. Herbie became almost a sixth member of the family. With my brother and sister I would sit high atop Herbie, looking out across our neighbourhood, dreaming all the weird and wonderful things that kids dream.

For the next 14 years this house would take on the truest sense of home. The walls and smells of a place in which you spend your mornings and nights almost become part of your DNA. At 182 Albert Street my family shared in a life that would be familiar to many. We enjoyed long, hot summers, school holidays and numerous slumber parties, but one particularly sad day is burnt into my memory.

It was decided that Herbie was listing on a dangerous angle, and there were concerns that he might fall – possibly onto my bedroom. Despite my best efforts through stages of appeal in our family's court of law, it was decided that Herbie had to be cut down. Without hesitation, I packed up the few possessions I had. With tears streaming down my face, my little legs carried me as far as I could go. Though this was only to the vacant block next door, my protest was enough to warrant a search party.

Although the murder of Herbie was a horrifying event, I decided that the paddock lacked the creature comforts I had become accustomed to in my first six years on the planet, so I trudged back home with a vow to never forget my old green-leafed friend. I also promised that I would never run away again.

After those warm and fuzzy times of childhood, I moved to the big city. As much as I loved the energy there, I didn't particularly enjoy the renting merry-go-round of small flats and an ever-changing cast and crew of flatmates. My sense of home had changed again: no longer was home a refuge, merely a place to keep your things.

Thankfully, the Kennel filled that void in these 'lost' years away from home. That sense of belonging is the greatest thing an organisation such as a football club can offer.

In more recent times, home has been a small cottage in North Fitzroy for me, my girl and Arthur. But with our little family about to increase by one in a few weeks, we need to find somewhere with a bit more space.

Home is ever-changing, and it is different for all of us. You can even have more than one. So while Arthur, Justine and I look for a three-bedroom house with a big gum tree out the front to call home for the next little while, I am still lucky enough to be able to rely on 417 Barkly Street, Footscray, as a home. The Kennel is not looking the best at the moment, but that's the thing with renovations – a little uncomfortable for a while, but in the end it will sparkle.

Just like my 14 years in Warragul, some years are tougher than others. This year at the Kennel has been one of difficulty, but unlike that little dog and a juvenile Robert Murphy, no one is running away. We are all going to stick it out – just like any good family does.

This column is dedicated to the memory of Herbie, possibly the greatest tree that ever lived.

23 August 2007

THINKING AMID
THE DRINKING

As I awoke from a brief catnap while travelling home in the front seat of my taxi on Monday evening, I was struck by two thoughts.

The first was that I had clearly had my fill at the day's wake. The other realisation that registered through the haze was that the rest of the country was probably enjoying finishing work, putting its collective feet up to watch the news and maybe enjoying a cold beer or chardonnay.

For the professional footballer, this day is unlike any other in the 365 that we tackle each year. It is a day spent in a parallel universe. A bit like *Lord of the Flies* if you added drinking games.

Mad Monday seems to have captured the imagination of the football public – a football public, I might add, that has an unquenchable thirst for information about how players spend their time away from the glare of the cameras. Year after year I am asked about the antics of Mad Monday, which is more or less just a day spent sitting in a pub with a bunch of blokes talking over the top of one another. The funny thing is that many of the people who are so fascinated actually do pretty much that very thing every Friday and Saturday night.

So what happens on Mad Monday? Is it just a day of scallywag antics? Or is it a necessary release of the tension that inevitably builds up over a long season?

After a season of disappointment, members of the eight teams that miss out on the finals get together at a designated watering hole for a day of male bonding. Nothing more, nothing less. Fast food, male hugging and the odd bit of beer-induced reflux are just a few of the standards on this day. It can be a day of embarrassment, but not humiliation.

Each club has its own Mad Monday laws. At the Bulldogs, it is always agreed that Chris Grant be the grand master; any dispute shall be judged finally by him, and any penalty is imposed at his discretion. Retiring players – Luke Darcy and Matthew Robbins – were given concessions this year, but by no means total immunity. As at most clubs, the first-year players had a lot asked of them, and each did himself proud.

The restrictions on what players can and can't do in modern football are immense. Alcohol, sleep and diet are closely monitored all year to maximise performance. When the season is over and 40 or so teammates in the prime of their lives are allowed to step away from the game for a few weeks, a pressure valve is released and these young men like to sit around over a well-earned beer and tell stories.

The same thing has gone on in this country for as long as the eyes of history can see. I'm sure our early settlers did something similar, and I can be pretty sure that the Anzacs enjoyed each other's company over a cold beer. Mad Monday has another name – and that is mateship. In this climate of scrutiny on players misbehaving, let us not forget that mateship is one of the cornerstones of this country and shouldn't be lost because of a few bad apples.

Football is the toughest sport going around, and your peers require you to push your body and mind further than maybe you thought possible. The only way people will undergo such strain with so much faith is due largely to bonding. Mad Monday, or whatever you want to call it, is just another example of the bonding each club tries to build, year in and year out.

I awoke from my slumber on Tuesday morning feeling a little fuzzy in the head, as I'm sure my teammates did. But the pain of a wretched season was not forgotten. That will take a few months to heal.

Even through all the silly games and immature jokes, there were quieter moments on Monday for reflection, and a realisation that we have a long and hard road ahead to get to where we want to go.

6 September 2007

2008

ROMANCE OF THE LITTLE LEAGUE

My name is Robert Murphy, and I'm addicted to romantic comedy movies. Boy oh boy, it feels good to finally say it out loud! I've been watching movies like *Notting Hill* and *When Harry Met Sally* for quite a few years now – away from the prying eyes of family and friends, of course, for fear of being cast out as a pansy. They have been my guilty pleasure.

The best way I can describe how much the addiction has taken hold is to tell you this: if Tom Hanks and Meg Ryan ever decide to saddle up again and do a sequel to *You've Got Mail*, I'd sleep out on the pavement to get the best seats. I know I've got issues, but at least I'm prepared to tackle them head-on.

People, this little admission is a look into the deepest and darkest recesses of my soul, and over the next few paragraphs I will try to explain what relevance it has to the state of footy at the moment.

One of my all-time favourite rom coms is the hugely popular (with housewives everywhere) *Love Actually*. In the opening scenes, the narrator (Hugh Grant, of course) talks about the perception that the world is a hard, cynical place, a place where romance, compassion and love can be lost amid the evils of the big, bad corporate world. Hugh goes on to say that whenever he hears such doom and gloom, he casts his mind to the departure gates of Heathrow airport, and all he sees is warm hugs and tears of loving affection. A love that is reserved for those closest to us.

As the rain flickered against my lounge room window on Sunday night, while my little family was huddled up watching *Love Actually* (again), it struck me how these same feelings can cross over to our great game. After another weekend of radio talkback complaining about umpiring decisions, on top of more television reporting on the politics of the game, it's easy to slip into a mood of doom and gloom, fearful that all the great things about our game are being lost.

Of course, this isn't true, and thankfully our game has so many gems to cherish that it's just a matter of keeping sight of them through the haze of negativity.

Grant's character talks of Heathrow's departure lounge in such glowing terms that it made me wonder: what, in football terms, is my Heathrow? After only a few seconds squinting through the haze, I saw lots of little people running around and a smile ran across my face.

The little league! If ever I feel myself going down Doom and Gloom Road, all I need do is think about the kiddies running around at half time, with nothing more on their minds than getting the ball and kicking it to their mates. If ever we needed a model of how the game should be played and ruled, it comes from this bunch of boys and girls.

They play with unbridled spirit. There is a distinct lack of emphasis on rules or tribunals; rather, there is a governing body of helpful parents who are more interested in the ethics of fair play than in how each boy or girl plays. The result is a harmonious spectacle.

As a wee lad growing up, I was lucky enough to play in the little league. A few memories from this day have not been dimmed one bit with time. After our minibus made the relatively short trip from Warragul to Waverley Park, I will never forget the feeling of running up the race and out onto the field in front of so many people. The other, more embarrassing memory from my big day in the little league is that I was playing for Hawthorn. Despite my loyalty to the Tigers at that time, I still endeavoured to wear the fetching combination of brown and gold with pride.

The main game that day was between the Hawks and Adelaide, so naturally the little league was contested by the same teams. Little kids have a funny little take on the world; not ones for the finer details on life, are they? Well, I certainly wasn't.

You see, I spent most of the game in a state of deep intrigue . . . I couldn't believe these other kids had come all the way from Adelaide to play a ten-minute game! My mum certainly wouldn't have let me fly over there to play!

It's a shame such wide-eyed wonder can be lost in the big, bad, grown-up world. In a week where it has been impossible not to be confronted by the Wayne Carey saga, we have received another reminder of just how much the adult we become is shaped by the child we are loved and encouraged to be.

As the rain falls this weekend and you stand in the outer

at half time with your hot pie and *Footy Record*, take a couple of minutes to watch the little league kids go about their stuff. It will be plain for you to see that the game is in great shape – as long as the kids are all right.

3 April 2008

FOOTY'S FIELD
OF DREAMS

Okay, it's Fantasy Football League time again! Please, check your coats and pessimism at the door on your way into the Field of Dreams, high up in the Hollywood Hills. And don't forget to grab your *Footy Record* and a hot pie of imagination.

After last year's rocking success with our team of rock stars, I thought we could do it all again, only this time without music. Instead, a motley crew of actors from our silver screens. I know you're all bursting to see who's made the line-up, so without further ado, we welcome . . .

THE BACK SIX

Robert De Niro: A real in-and-under type. His connections with the underworld are well known but he says it's all above board. Took much persuading to get him to the club, with president Marlon Brando revealing: 'I made him an offer he couldn't refuse.'

Anthony Hopkins: Feared competitor who likes to take control of the club barbecue; his burgers after training are legendary. Of his secret recipe, Hopkins says: 'It's all to do with the cut of meat.'

Quentin Tarantino: Has brought a hard edge to a team of sensitive souls. Lack of interest in marks, kicks and handballs is supplemented by his thirst for the contest and love of on-field violence. Responsible for more blood rule send-offs than anyone in the game.

Russell Crowe: Was reinstated as a player after a brief stint as coach, when his tendency to smash phones was deemed excessive by President Brando. Russell's focus at training and during games gives him a prickly demeanour, but his teammates love his gladiatorial courage.

Mickey Rourke: Former Rising Star winner back after a sabbatical chasing a boxing dream. Has become the face of the club, although the face looks a little weird after some post-season surgery. Fond of the booze and ciggies on the end-of-season trips.

John Travolta: His twinkle toes have the ability to dazzle fans one minute and leave them frustrated the next. Has benefited from teammate Tarantino's unselfish play. Missed last Saturday night's game with a fever but is right to play this week.

ON-BALLERS

Hilary Swank: A real tomboy who is not above using her fists to make her feelings known. Former best-and-fairest winner who relies more on determination than finesse.

Steven Seagal: Only rivalled by Jack Nicholson for his accomplishments on the field. Has a swag of awards and trophies and the respect of his peers and the football public. Versatile and elegant, Seagal is an artist with substance and panache.

Daniel Craig: Rookie who has taken all before him in the number seven jersey. His emergence from the reserves was pretty amazing, but his emergence from the bay at Port Melbourne last week in his blue euro togs had hearts fluttering.

Sienna Miller: Has played a lot of games in a short period of time at this level, many of them without her jumper on. This has had some critics up in arms, but the male-dominated football public has welcomed the approach as a healthy form of individuality.

Daniel Day Lewis: Reclusive big man who famously forgoes the regular season and plays only finals. Still makes the most of his time on the ground; asked who he'd like to thank after winning last year's Norm Smith Medal, he replied: 'My left foot.'

Tom Cruise: A few good men have tried to stop this former top gun, but his powers have dimmed in recent seasons. Got into hot water with his teammates for imposing on them a leadership program that borders on a religious cult.

FORWARDS

Steve Buscemi: Not so much a sneaky forward as a creepy forward. Not on the huge salaries of some teammates, but always adds something to the side.

James Dean: Icon whose reputation is sure to get even bigger following retirement. Stylish and skilful with his hands. His ability to kick with both feet is well publicised. A real rebel in his heyday.

Tom Hanks: Versatile champion who just keeps on running. His field kicking is exceptional, but you never quite know what you might get in front of goal (much like a box of chocolates). Recent criticism from our very own Robert Walls has been that he plays soft football when Meg Ryan is alongside him.

Jack Nicholson: Had a stint as coach after Crowe, in which he liked to sit at ground level, or 'courtside'. Back playing now, and his credentials are quite simply as good as it gets. Has proven a hit in the social club with the ladies, too. So good, he makes up our entire full-forward line.

THE BENCH

Mel Gibson: Local lad who had a mad start to his career before becoming a lethal weapon up forward. Currently suspended under vilification laws.

Ben Mendelsohn: A local star who hasn't played at this level, and probably won't play this week, but his form in the lower grades is such that this sports journo would like to see his name up in lights.

Kevin Costner: Would have been left out after numerous howlers, but sneaks in because he built the home ground.

Hugh Grant: Burst onto the scene as a youngster with his divine brown hair. His soft efforts and lack of versatility have some calling for a demotion back to local club Notting Hill.

CLUB PHYSIO

Scarlett Johansson: Her position came under scrutiny due to an epidemic of osteitis pubis immediately after her appointment. An inquiry revealed little as the results were lost in translation. With Woody Allen on her CV, she can walk into any club she wants.

1 May 2008

THE TUNNEL
OF LOVE

'I'm not a groupie . . . I'm a band aid,' said Kate Hudson's character, Penny Lane, in *Almost Famous*, trying to tell her younger admirer that she wasn't on the hunt for sexual conquests, but a true fan who 'dug' the music. It's not for me to judge whether Penny was true to her word, but she sure did like those musicians. I've had a few Penny Lane moments of my own this past week – without the sexual conquests, of course.

Having been given the honour of representing Victoria, I had butterflies for the entire drive to training at the MCG, and they didn't let up until Sunday morning as I bade my farewell to Camp Victoria.

In a way, most footballers are like Penny. They are fans – fans of the game and of the great players. To be rubbing shoulders with the game's elite was, as you would expect for a fan, quite thrilling. But, like with royal protocol, there is a certain dignity one must keep in the company of the greats, so I put my autograph book away for the week.

Preparing for training with my new teammates and coaches was exciting, and a little awkward. It's an unusual situation to be in, whereby everyone knows who everyone else is but they've never met (apart from on the field of play).

Small talk not being a strong suit of mine, I shuffled around with eyes aimed low, looking for my locker, only pausing to reflect when I put my jumper on. Footy is a ride of ups and downs, but this was certainly a nice moment that I'll keep forever. With my club skipper, Brad Johnson, incapacitated, I suddenly felt like I was in the school playground with the big kids and with no big brother to look out for me.

Thankfully, the big kids in this playground were not the bullying type, and once the footballs were brought out the tension eased. The power of that ball, I mused – it never ceases to amaze.

Contrary to what some of my early coaches might think, I've always enjoyed football training. It's much like lunchtime at school, when you'd run around kicking and handballing with your mates until the bell rang.

Running onto the MCG last week on a frosty Thursday morning with the best players in the league was a tingle-worthy moment. Even so, I was plagued by a lingering feeling of guilt. Was this a case of football infidelity? Was I cheating on my wife – the Bulldogs – with this glamorous and exciting mistress – Victoria?

I decided to try and make some friends to avoid the confronting idea that I was an adulterer. Footballers and football clubs are relatively similar wherever you go, and the Victorian camp was no different. You just need some time to find your role in the social landscape of the team. A footy team needs a certain amount of roles to be played out – and I don't mean backs, forwards and mids.

There has to be a class clown, someone to break the ice with the group and to happily make fun of himself to put others at ease. Brendan Fevola plays this part as if he was born to it.

Then, of course, there is the chatty little fella who keeps the mood up all the time – Luke Power took to this role with consummate ease.

And when it came to who would be the boss, someone to take charge of morale and direction, it was left to the big boy from up north, J. Brown. I say 'boy' with my tongue firmly in my cheek, for if anyone was to be described as a man, then surely it's him. With dangerous levels of testosterone coursing through him, he has the rare ability to influence others through his very presence.

These are just a few of the roles that had to be quickly filled by the time we ran onto the park. The freak, the superstar and the ladies man would all be filled by the likes of S. Johnson, C. Judd and J. Selwood, respectively.

As for the team's weirdo, I'm not really sure we had one. I heard the boys talking about it at times, but the conversation always fizzled out when I walked into the room, which I thought was odd.

Anyway, after a couple more training sessions and official functions with my mistress, there was one last rendezvous to go. Not in the back corner of a dark, seedy bar. No, I chose to take my affair into the spotlight – on a Saturday night under lights at the MCG.

Afterwards, we retired to a local pub to chat over the week, which was great. Stories and laughs carried well into the night.

When the Dream Team boys showed up, the stories and laughter only got bigger.

Slipping back into my bed this week with my wife in red, white and blue, it was hard to escape the guilt of my weekend's dirty deeds. I must say, it's nice to be back with the missus, and there's nothing like your own bed, is there? But I will never forget my whirlwind week with the mistress in the blue dress with a white V down the front.

15 May 2008

The after-match function was actually a lot more spirited
than the game itself, and the drinking went into the wee hours of
the morning. A tribute, if you like, to the State of Origin
teams of the past. In a room full of Premierships, Brownlows
and Coleman Medals, the bloke everyone wanted to have
a beer with was Matthew 'Richo' Richardson. Few players have
entertained other players as much as the great Tiger.

A FAIR SHAKE

As I get older, I can feel myself becoming more Irish, and I welcome this reconnection to my heritage. The rolling green hills are talking to me, beckoning, calling on me to become who I really am. A Murphy. An Irishman. A pale, brown-haired Paddy.

My late teens and early 20s were a time of experimentation; like most young men, I tried a few things to see what best suited me. After a brief dalliance with tips in my hair and a couple of visits to the solarium, it became quite obvious that whoever I was trying to be was not myself, only someone I thought might appeal to others.

Over time, the tips grew out, and the tan that never really took faded away. I was left to find another path. But, as they say, sometimes to go forward you must know where it is you've come from.

Having been suspended last week by the match review panel for my heinous crime, I felt as if not only was there a one-week penance to serve, but also that I was being forced back into the shackles my ancestors wore as they boarded the First Fleet. All week, as I passed the time reading Rousseau, the steel of the handcuffs and leg irons pressed against my flesh as a reminder that I wouldn't be joining my teammates to take on the Saints.

As I sat and watched my boys strut their stuff, the welts on my ankles and wrists were suffering under the heavy burden. At game's end, as I stood off the playing group and watched the boys belt out 'Sons of the West', I had my suspension lifted – and the shackles went with it. With my arms now able to move freely, and my legs to stretch properly, I did what any decent Irishman would do – I went to the pub.

There was plenty to celebrate. I was a free man, of course, the Doggies had won, and it was also the eve of my 26th birthday. Having all sat down to enjoy a meal and a couple of drinks together, we raised our glasses to say cheers. Well, that set Mum off. 'Do you know why we do that?' she asked.

'Do what?' I replied.

'The way we all show each other our drinks and then gently have them touch all the other glasses at the table.'

Dear old Mum is a bottomless well of little derivations and pearls of wisdom. Some are genuine and some we are pretty sure she just makes up. But her thoughts about the tradition of cheers-ing intrigued me.

She claims the reason we bang our drinks together comes from a time when noblemen would have a meal together to discuss money, war and politics. Remembering how brutal this time was, these men would bang cups of wine to demonstrate that what they were drinking was indeed the same, and no foul play had taken place with poisons and the like.

Our colliding glasses jogged a thought about the game that day. Watching from the stands, I observed how another traditional greeting was holding up. I noticed that nobody shook hands with his opponent at the start of the game – or if anyone had, it was done so discreetly that I'd missed it.

It's a topic I've thought about a bit. I have always been a hand-shaker; I'm not really sure why I like the ritual, but I always did it – in much the same way I 'cheers' my drinks.

But now I fear the handshake is being pushed out of our game. As footballers, we are in the business of not showing any vulnerability. Often this is to our detriment, but in the macho world of the AFL those who choose not to shake before a game are deemed to possess the dominant gene over those who think it's a nice bit of sportsmanship that should be maintained.

The shakers are wary that if they offer their hand to a non-shaker, this will relinquish the perception that, once the siren goes, it's war. Anyone who sees shaking as a sign of softness need only look at Brett Kirk and ask why he still shakes his opponent's hand before they bounce the ball. He is as tough and respected as they come.

I have become a non-shaker in recent seasons, and it bothers me. After thinking about it this week, I've decided to campaign for the return of the handshake.

I may not know why we 'cheers' our glasses, but I know why I used to shake my opponent's hand – to wish him the best of luck and to let him know that I will play as hard and as fair as I'm able. If that's too 'vulnerable' for the non-shakers, then I guess I'll just be left hanging.

12 June 2008

A VISION SPLENDID

There is something about matches played in the twilight timeslot that throws me out completely. I haven't quite worked out why, but when I arrive home to have dinner it feels weird, like the first day of daylight saving, only a lot worse.

As is customary in this weekly column, I like to brush down the sideburns, swing by the record store for the obligatory '60s soundtrack, before heading back on the train to the early '90s to steal a piece of my childhood. It's then sprinkled with a little AFL, just to make it more palatable for the sports pages.

Well, not today. It's time to grow up. Actually, in light of the twilight games and the inevitable twilight zone backlash that follows, I thought we should strap on our space boots, jump in Marty McFly's DeLorean and head back to the future!

Setting the scene: 25 June 2018: Robert Murphy is still an *Age* columnist after retiring from the Western Bulldogs in 2014, crippled by gout. He's still flogging the old formula – starting each column with rock 'n' roll lyrics, talking about his childhood, etc. His fans, while loyal, are dwindling. His critics are growing by the day.

One noticeable change is that he never mentions his sausage dog, Arthur, since his untimely demise. Famously, Arthur was scared stiff of water and would never walk over a puddle, let alone go for a swim. But Arthur confronted his H2O fears, taking off one day across Bass Strait, never to be seen again.

It's a sore point for the columnist, who claims he never tried to replace his little four-legged friend, despite purchasing two more dachshunds and calling them Marthur and Arthur Mk II.

'I've got a car, I've got a big, black, shiny car . . .' God only knows how the kids listen to this stuff, but as Shannon Noll sits atop the charts, I thought I'd try to appeal to the masses in a desperate attempt to stay hip.

'Better than that Mick Jagger s—t you play at home, Dad,' moans ten-year-old Jarvis Murphy.

Anyway, folks, back to the business of footy, footy, footy. As I travelled down to Launceston on the weekend to see my old team, the Doggies, take on the Tigers, I couldn't help but feel a little forlorn. The game itself was no great shakes, and even though I was cheered a little to see the Bulldogs escape with a two-point win over the old rival from Punt Road, there were still things that fuelled my pessimism about the modern game.

Bulldog veteran Ayce Cordy, a shining light for the Dogs over the last ten seasons, was reported for making eye contact with an umpire, and with points hanging over his head from a similar incident two weeks ago, he looks to be in danger of missing next week's clash with Gold Coast. A big fan of water slides, Ayce is understood to be shattered.

Back to the game itself. I sat with my old teammate Daniel Giansiracusa, and despite claims from the experts that football is quicker, the players tougher and the skills at an all-time high, we both agreed that the current payers are not as tough as we were, and have decided to publicly criticise the Dogs on talkback radio – not to self-promote, you understand, just to help the club improve.

Veteran Bulldogs coach Rodney Eade was upbeat after the win, but came under scrutiny for this quote: 'We didn't do the brand any harm today.' Eade was fined $10,000 for breaking rule 14.7, which states: 'Any use of the word "brand" shall be sanctioned due to its condescending nature – just call it your football club.'

Terry Wallace was, as usual, upbeat despite the narrow loss, but was lucky to escape an AFL sanction of his own for describing a Cleve Hughes mark as a 'catch'.

You'll all remember that, back in 2013, there were some words and phrases highlighted in this column that I believed were hurting the fabric of football. On that glorious day, accompanied by my team of lawyers, I marched into AFL House in an attempt to have words such as 'brand', 'catch' and 'franchise', and phrases such as 'is he a champion?', 'kicks it from outside the paint', 'they didn't come to play', 'he's gotten ahead of himself' and 'growth markets' outlawed. Our chests heaved with pride when Andrew Demetriou banned their use forever.

As I said earlier, the game itself was of no great standard, but it was remarkable for one reason. Brad Johnson lining up for his 500th game was always going to be cause for celebration out west, but to have the milestone fall on the day his son Jack made his debut in red, white and blue would have to rank as the second-most amazing day for the club this year.

Second, of course, to drillers striking oil beneath Whitten Oval, a discovery that left the club with untold riches and also lowered petrol to a reasonable $3.56 a litre. With the Bulldogs now cashed up, it looks as though they will be purchasing the Collingwood Football Club and renting the Lexus Centre back to it.

26 June 2008

DEBRIEF ENCOUNTERS

Before last week, a good friend of mine, Jon, was a devout vegetarian. Turned off by the taste of meat from a young age, his choice to bypass such culinary delights as chops, sausages, steak and the great Australian lamb roast had set him apart from the pack. I suspect growing up in Tasmania made him an even rarer commodity.

But something in ol' Jon Boy must have changed significantly, and at some point he made the decision to dip his toe into the pool shared by us meat eaters. I say 'dip his toe' out of respect, but in reality he has jumped off the top tower and made a rather big splash. No sooner was he nibbling at a piece of chicken than he was hoeing into a meatlovers' pizza and ordering steaks with the strict instruction that there be no salads on the side. Hats off to you, Jon, I say – we have to do what makes us happy or we shall perish.

I got a lot out of my friend's revelation, as it highlighted something that I could put in my training bag to help deal

with the fact that my boys have gone down in similar fashion
the past two weeks running. Things can change quickly, sometimes without our control. And sometimes – as with Jon – our
actions can totally change our course and fortunes.

This week's mission for my Bulldogs is to get back on the
winners' list and, more importantly, to play the type of football we showed earlier in the year. And there is no better side
to test yourself against than the Swans.

Football's most famous song, 'Up There Cazaly', touches
on how vulnerable we are to the dark side of the game's personality: 'There are days when you could give it up, there are
days when you could fly!' This game tests you all the time;
anyone who's played or loved it can relate to that.

In the minutes straight after a loss, sitting slumped against
the wall, the mind races with all sorts of emotions and questions: 'What could I have done differently?' Being called in
for the post-match debrief with the coach can make for a tense
few minutes.

With a nickname like 'Rocket', you'd think our coach's voice
might have torn the paint off the walls after our poor showing
in Sunday's second half. The master of surprise and psychology,
within a few minutes Rocket had pointed out some things we
needed to address, and then quickly lifted the emotions of the
room and the club by focusing on the upcoming challenges.
Never once did he raise his voice.

Over my time in the game, this post-match 'chat' has been
known to escalate into a verbal spray. While Rocket has mostly
confined himself to a shake of the head and a 'Disappointing,
Robert', one particular post-match address I witnessed as a
youngster under Terry Wallace will not be forgotten in a hurry.

After being soundly beaten by Carlton (again), we were called into the meeting room in the bowels of Optus Oval. My teammates and I looked up to see a whiteboard that was, to me, confusing. Under two headings – 'Volunteers' and 'Conscripts' – were spread the names of the players.

The natural reaction is to scan for your own name, isn't it? Well, mine was under 'Conscripts', and for a brief moment I thought this was a good thing. I was wrong. 'Plough' had conjured up a review of us individually, as if the game was a war. How you played was to determine whether you volunteered for battle with honour, or were a conscript who had to be called upon and had less conviction than the volunteers.

After some time, during which Plough made his way through the list, it was my turn to be 'sprayed'. I was sitting on the floor in the front row – big mistake. I was only a metre away from him. He detailed to me and my teammates how my lack of honour as a soldier had been like an opposition soldier taking my own knife off me and stabbing me with it. He even stepped forward to show me how it was done – pulling my imaginary knife from its imaginary sheath and driving it into me with the words, 'Bang – you're dead!'

This review went on for what seemed like hours, but was probably less than one. After we heard about other teammates being 'MIA', and some being left on the battlefield alongside a couple of generals who had fought manfully, finally it was over. The creativity and theatrics that Plough often brought to the table was too much for one assistant coach, and I could see his shoulders shaking with giggles in the back corner.

I was in no mood for giggles. I felt ashamed in front of my teammates (or soldiers).

The fact that Daniel Cross still pretends to stab me, yelling, 'Bang – you're dead!' shows that day will stay with me for a very long time. And the fact that I still think about it probably tells me that it worked, as I never want to let my fellow soldiers down again.

Those days, like the past couple of weeks, pass. And the wonderful thing is that, unlike the volunteers and conscripts who didn't return from battle, we get a chance to turn it around.

31 July 2008

SOMETHING'S IN THE AIR

As I woke up to begin the new week, this Monday felt just like any other. Still a little battle-sore from the weekend's game, I embarked on my morning ritual of coffee and newspaper.

Something felt a little off, though. It wasn't an obvious something, like waking up on the couch instead of in your bed. This was a more subtle change and it took me most of the morning to figure it out. For one thing, Arthur was very keen to go for a walk, which is quite a dramatic change to his winter routine of steadfastly refusing to brave the cold, wet ground.

After devouring the brew that had been so lovingly made by my coffee queen, Martha, I set about making swift work of the paper. Still, a feeling lingered that some greater power was at work. I wasn't too concerned, though, as this strange feeling carried a positive air, and none of the dread you feel when you suspect you have forgotten a team meeting, a la Andrew Symonds. So I kept on reading and gradually made my way to the back of the paper.

As each page of the sports section was done with, I began to realise a couple of things. The first was that half the teams in the AFL had been eliminated! This was news to me. Having been in the AFL system for the best part of a decade, I thought I had a good grasp on the lay of the land. Sure, I'd heard about a thing called 'finals', but I thought it had something to do with a Mad Monday drinking game.

As I sat there in my kitchen, stunned, I felt an excitement bubble up inside me. My boys in the red, white and blue were about to embark on something new and exciting. Maybe that was why Arthur had a spring in his step. He's a huge Bulldogs fan, as you know, and the past few years have been tough on him, just as they have been on all our supporters.

Checking my phone to get the exact time of my epiphany, I noticed a couple of missed calls from an old teammate, Nathan Brown, left at around 2 am. Another drunken rendition of the Tigers' theme song awaiting me on my voicemail, I mused. I have never felt so healthy or so un-hungover (if I might be allowed to stretch the English language to my every whim) as I did in that moment.

So, finals. What are they all about, then? Having played 148 games but not one in September, I had to get a grip on what lay ahead of me and my Dogs. I googled them, and even asked complete strangers to give me their quick summation of what I could expect.

My favourite explanation came from an elderly gentleman named Ted, who was walking his dog in my neighbourhood.

'What are finals all about?' I asked.

'Very much like oysters for you, I'd imagine.'

Puzzled, I asked Ted what he meant.

'Well, I imagine the first time you tried an oyster, you looked at it and examined it quite closely. Maybe even thought to yourself that it looked a little scary. But overriding that was a fascination and curiosity fuelled by people telling you how divine they are. Am I right?'

It was as if Ted had looked straight into my soul and perfectly encapsulated the emotions the prospect of finals football was bringing out in me.

As Arthur and I strode briskly back home, it was almost time to hop in the car and head to training. Loading up the Mini with my footy bag and other bits and pieces, I noted one of my front tyres was a little flat. It would have to be pumped up if I was going to make it to training, and the finals.

The Mini has played Kit to my David Hasselhoff all season, gently serving as a reliable donkey and also a voice of reason and philosophical guidance. All year the Mini's form has mirrored the fortunes of the Dogs – in the groove and moving with swift precision for most of the season, only to stall a few weeks back.

The Mini told me what it thought of our drop in form in no uncertain manner – by wrapping itself in toilet paper. (Readers will recall 'toilet papergate'; having been unable to unearth a culprit, I can only conclude the wounds were self-inflicted, a 'Mini protest' at our mini-slump.) So I wasn't about to ignore its cry for help, and headed straight for the service station.

Finals, I have decided, are all about the new and the exciting. Spring weather, fresh air in your tyres and a couple of oysters to wash it all down.

4 September 2008

2009

CHANGES APLENTY, BUT LIFE'S CONSTANTS SHINE

The more things change, the more they stay the same. I've no idea who first uttered that, but they should step forward and take a bow because it's brilliant. It might not make sense but it does make beautiful poetry.

Not everything has to make sense, does it? I was never much good at maths and science at school; I never had the answers, and in those subjects it's all about answers. I was much more comfortable sitting in an art room looking out the window and talking about space, asking pointless questions that weren't meant to be answered.

In a footy sense, 'the more things change, the more they stay the same' has never rung truer. The game is on the verge of a breakdown, so I keep hearing – ugly footy and negative tactics, rolling zones, clusters and the like. It's not enough that the front of the paper is full of doom and gloom, now it's spread to the back.

I'd like this particular space in the paper to be a bit more 'glass half-full', and I fully expect the game to sort itself out and be as good as it's ever been. No matter how many strategies and rule changes the game endures, it will always come out shiny because at its heart it is beautiful and unique, a game played by bodies of all shapes and sizes chasing an odd-shaped ball.

Chaos will always play an integral part in our game. The answers are never going to be as simple as two plus two, and we're best to throw out the maths and enjoy footy for what it is. No matter what the trends of the day, you still have to get the ball first and use it better than the other team. Do that, and most of the time you'll win; all the other stuff becomes blotter.

So what has changed and what's stayed the same since we last spoke? My holidays got off to an ordinary start – post-season surgery is always a bit of a downer, aside from the few moments of pure bliss you have before going under. Not so good coming out of theatre, mind you, in pain and utterly confused.

There were first steps – mine post-surgery, wobbly and painful. Then Jarvis, taking his own long-awaited first paces at the ripe old age of 17 months – wobbly too, but funny.

Next, Arthur finally confronted his fear of the water, plucking up the courage to walk through his first puddle. Cute. Then, as Jarvis, his mum and I and a couple of teammates set sail off Barwon Heads for a spot of fishing, with Arthur looking on longingly from the pier, our little sausage dog took a leap of faith and, to our horror, was suddenly tumbling down the river, out of sorts and out of breath. Strange dog. Courageous, but strange.

And then there was marriage, the biggest leap of all in many ways, but a much more enjoyable one than Arthur's off the pier. Jarvis's mum is some gal, so I've taken extraordinary steps to show my commitment to her, and will now be known as Bob Quigley. Brian Lake, eat your heart out.

Along with the new, there have been comebacks, too. The bronzed playboy who had it all and threw it away is back where he belongs, on top, looking a little life-weary (as you would after being put through the wringer for a year or two) but appearing to have lost little of the magic. Welcome back, Mickey Rourke.

Despite my disappointment at Mickey missing out on an Oscar, it was heart-warming to see such a star – with talent and charisma to burn – return to the main stage to delight the masses. Kinda reminds me of someone else who'll be having a run tonight. A great chance to silence the sideshow of intrusion on his dining rituals, and show us why the fascination started in the first place. Best of luck to him.

There is a moment every year when this city changes gear and finds the slower pace of winter. Arriving home this week, I think I felt it – something in the air, and also the way the light had softened on the bricks of my little neighbourhood. Winter has always been a better fit for Melbourne, I think.

The football season feeds on a huge amount of oxygen, and its ups and downs, wins and losses, glory and pain can leave you feeling a little short of breath if you don't step back every so often and inhale. But it's gripping enough to bring people out in their droves, to fly a flag and yell at the players and umpires, even though they know we can't really hear them.

Gee, it's good to have the footy back. I hope 2009 belongs to my Bulldogs and brings good weather for ducks.

26 March 2009

THEM'S THE BRAKES

How much does your car know about you? Mine told me this week that I am vulnerable, and it scared the life out of me.

I've had my Mini Cooper for a couple of years now, and we've had our ups and downs. Who could forget Toilet Paper-gate last year? (It turned out to be Gilbee, Griffen and Higgins. Sorry for the eggs, Will.) Over this time, I've sometimes felt as if the Mini was talking to me in its own way. Every time it would break down (often), I would break down soon after. This happened more times than I'd care to admit, and became a bit of a running joke.

A few months back, a light started flashing on my dash. Being the engine fanatic that I am, I looked it up in the manual to get to the root of the problem. The back right tyre was in some kind of distress. And, wouldn't you know it, my right leg was sending out a few distress signals of its own at the very same time!

For the entire pre-season I drove to and from training with that light flashing at me: 'Your back right tyre is vulnerable.'

Vulnerability is not something usually associated with footballers, is it? Yet human nature is such that we are all vulnerable in some way. In many ways, it's what binds us: we can find comfort in the fact that our flaws give us common ground, no matter who we are.

So unless footballers really aren't human, it seems logical to me that the vulnerability is there, only its signs are being hidden behind a macho bravado that has been handed down from one generation of footballers to the next.

From a very young age it is drilled into us, with fathers or coaches passing on the age-old adage of not showing the opposition – or anyone else, for that matter – a hint of weakness. Winded? Stand up tall and run it out. Feel like crying? Pour water over your face to conceal the tears.

Only last week, Jonathan Brown mentioned the possibility of chopping his injured little finger off because little fingers are much like tonsils – easily done without. It's not hard to imagine the big boy from Warrnambool doing just that – he is genuinely tough, as we're all expected to be. But maybe we can strike a balance, and reach a point after the boots have come off where we can be more of an open book.

I love tradition in football. But I think this particular tradition of denial is quite possibly holding us back as a group. People from outside the reaches of football are quick to remind me that footballers in general are quite thick and boorish. In recent years, the steady flow of unsavoury off-field incidents has given the naysayers more fuel to heap on the fire.

I suspect this image hasn't been helped by the lack of an outlet for us to show vulnerability. Our century-old tradition of chest-out invincibility is not in sync with modern society.

The football media is geared heavily towards a quick head-line and a negatively slanted dissection of a team or individual. This hasn't helped – players who confront the media are fearful of diverting from the club's party line and becoming another human headline – or, worse still, giving an answer that, despite its honesty, reveals a potential weak spot. You can see why we've come up with an almanac of clichés.

As my Dogs went to work on Monday, I was sent off to do the rounds of radio and TV. Walking up to the broadcast area, I went through a quick rehearsal in my head and strapped myself into the harness as if I was about to walk the high wire. It's a sport of balance – try to remain vaguely interesting, but also be mindful not to show any chinks in your armour.

At some point during each interview the topic of my knee injury came up, and each time I gave a vaguely general answer with a hint of positivity. Behind the eyes, though, it's a point of real vulnerability that I felt compelled to keep to myself. Of course I'm vulnerable – I even have the scar to prove it.

With my work on the high wire complete, I sat and enjoyed the Dogs doing the business, then drove home to ponder for the umpteenth time where my football was headed. Time to get rid of the Mini, I thought, and maybe pick up an old clas-sic. So, sitting outside the front door now is a glorious old '66 XP Falcon – with bench seats!

I knew we were made for each other from my very first test drive, when I accidentally left the handbrake on for the entire trip. It was embarrassing but somehow fitting – I feel like I've had my own handbrake on all summer. When I picked up Frankie this week, the first thing I did was make sure the brake was off, and she drove just beautifully.

Aussie rules is no different to an old XP – both could benefit greatly from taking the handbrake off and showing ourselves for what we really are.

16 April 2009

AN ALL-AUSTRALIAN TEAM FOR ALL AUSTRALIANS

With Anzac Day still fresh in our minds and winter descending on our grand old town, what better time to warm the heart by paying homage to our national icons. So here it is, the Australian All-Australian team.

Stand up tall, take your cap off and put your hand over your heart as we belt out the national anthem before watching our fellows (plus a few products, the odd landmark and a horse) burst through the banner.

Just don't scream that 'Aussie, Aussie, Aussie' crap if you can help it. Uluru hates it.

BACKS

Humphrey B. Bear: Veteran defender who has always been a bear of few words, but crucially a bear of few goals against. Flat-out refusal to wear shorts has landed him in all manner of strife with officials. Has kept quiet on his motives for this.

Captain Cook: Skipper who has always fought hard for his crew. Miserly defence has kept the ship on an even keel. Good hands, kicks with both fleet.

Dicky Knee: Seems to be battling an injury of some sorts, but the club is keeping it hush-hush.

Sir Les Patterson: Scruffy half-back who has been a consistent performer for many years. A real favourite with the members for his antics in the social club. Untidy by hand and foot – untidy in general, come to mention it – his best footy now seems behind him.

Dame Edna: Star junior from Moonee Ponds has failed to deliver thus far. Off-season rumours of a trade to the Possums haven't endeared her to supporters. Should benefit from having Patterson as a sidekick in '09.

Sharon Strzelecki: Boiled lollies to chocolates story. Languishing in the reserves last year, now looks a picture of health. Squeezed out her hero, Shane Warne, for the final defensive post. (Didn't stop her trying to pash Warnie at training, mind you.)

CENTRES

Cathy Freeman: Automatic selection in a decorated midfield, simply cos she's free, cos she can play, and cos she's really, really fast.

Uluru: Permanent fixture of the midfield who did a Max Rooke over summer and changed name. We know what we'll get from this champion – not quick, but good luck in pushing off the ball.

Lionel Rose: Against the odds he has acquitted himself beautifully since being elevated from the rookie list to become a star of this team. Sharp on his feet and even sharper with his fists.

FORWARDS

Don Bradman: Famously used to handball his football against a water tank. Handball efficiency of 99.94 per cent speaks for itself.

Chesty Bonds: Favourite son. Plenty of overseas teams have tried to poach him but he has remained loyal. Introduction of a 17th licence in China this year poses a possible threat, but he wouldn't leave us in our hour of need, would he?

Bindi Irwin: Precocious number one draft pick who the kids can't get enough of. Destined to outlast us all.

Vegemite: Tiny goalsneak who just keeps on keeping on. Doesn't need much of it to go well. Sat on Toast's head recently to take mark of the year.

Nicole Kidman: Modern-day marvel in the Matthew Richardson mould – appears to be ageing in reverse. Concern over how she'll handle Keith Urban being dropped this week. If only his run at the ball was as straight as his hair.

Skippy: Team player obsessed with helping teammates out of tricky situations. Leads competition in blocks, smothers, shepherds, spoils and calling the stretcher for help. Has a huge leap. Teammates follow her lead, despite failure to understand her.

RUCKS

Ned Kelly: Modern-day Ben Hudson, with full beard to match.

Hardness around stoppages has created a gang mentality among teammates. Decision-making can seem unusual, but put it down to his unconventional protective headwear.

Phar Lap: 'Horse', as teammates know him, can run all day. 'He's got a heart as big as . . . as, um . . . what was that name again?' his coach said last week.

Kylie: Insists on being called 'Minogue' these days. Diminutive rover will have them spinning around in her wake. Tiny shorts are almost as revealing as Humphrey's complete lack of shorts, prompting Les Patterson to ponder: 'I couldn't get her out of my head!'

INTERCHANGE

Weet-Bix: Recruited in trade week after draft picks were thrown in to sweeten the deal.

Elle Macpherson: Outspoken views on life and spirituality have exhausted all to breaking point – except Les Patterson.

Molly Meldrum: Do yourself a favour, and get a seat to watch this kid play. Post-football future in recruiting beckons.

Gum Tree: This lanky legend was destined for the Hall of Fame. Cut down in his prime.

COACH

'Weary' Dunlop: Rugby union convert whose courage and compassion are unrivalled.

30 April 2009

BLESS THE
HEALING HANDS

It's funny that, of all the injuries I've had during games, when I'm asked to recall what went through my head at the precise moment, my perception of the incident is very different to what the camera tells us.

When Anthony Rocca snapped me in half like a Christmas bonbon, I couldn't really recall anything other than hearing a sickening crunch. So I was quite surprised when club doctor and Bay 13 icon Gary Zimmerman gave my knee the once over, and it was the doc who became quite upset as he told me that my season was shot. I was actually feeling a little embarrassed, and pretty keen to get off the ground, truth be told. For me, the tears would come later.

A pesky hamstring strain is nowhere near comparable to that level of distress, but the weekend's game still tossed my mind about again. How bad is it? Somewhere between a 'stinger' and a trip to Germany, it seems.

Hamstring strains are as much a part of the game as

liniment and half-time oranges – they are hardly in the category of catastrophe. But at that precise moment when those tiny fibres tear, it does feel like your leg and football life are ripped in two.

It's usually only a few moments before some perspective reappears, but those seconds are pretty dark for the player – and, I imagine, for the medical staff, who by this stage are on the battlefield (minus their donkeys) to take one of their own into their care.

I must say I had a premonition that it wasn't going to be my day. I'm no Robert Langdon (of *Da Vinci Code* fame), but symbolism is something I often find myself searching for.

You can imagine my horror on Saturday when a pigeon waddled up next to me during the warm-up and promptly died. To be honest, I didn't take a pulse, but as we alerted our match-day staff to the freak occurrence it became apparent that the poor old pigeon wouldn't see any more Bulldog games.

As I limped off the ground at the end of the first quarter, I wondered if the precise moment of my injury coincided with the pigeon's last breath. Morbid? Yes, but the minutes after an injury are a wild time filled with lunacy and sailor talk.

I've often thought about football's dry sense of humour, and 'the pigeon incident' has only supported these feelings. Sitting glumly on the bench, I received another reminder when a small boy stuck his head around our dugout, pointed at the scoreboard and said, 'Don't worry, Bob! You're still coming fourth in the dream team!'

These days, a player's football season is all about effort and recovery – the effort is on show for all to see on game day, but the recovery side comes in many shapes and sizes. It's not the technology I'm interested in, though, it's the people whose caring hands help players overcome or manage injuries

There's not much a player won't try to get himself fit to play, and I've come across some special people whose hands have helped me recover over the years. If you're looking for the heart of any football club, just make your way to the medical room. The spirit of 'Weary' Dunlop lives on in a very real sense in our great game in those who bandage, soothe and carry the players on and off the field of play.

The medical staff at the Bulldogs have been the players' backbone for a hundred years, but there are also a host of other carers outside the four walls who make a living using their hands to heal us.

I've spent more than enough time in the Bulldogs' blood-pump room to think about the importance of a good medical team. The heart is often a sanctuary free from the politics and intensity that rage around – and sometimes within – a football club. Seeing the Tigers under siege this week brought back memories of a similar time at the Bulldogs a few years back, and I wondered whether their cardiovascular system was a place of calm and empathy, like ours has always been. My gut tells me it would be, as at the heart of things most football clubs beat similarly.

Healing has many faces. My peeps have been in the wars this week, and we had to take an unscheduled trip to the Royal Children's Hospital. How bad was it? Similar to my 'string, in a way.

As our little family sat in the waiting area, I thought about how the children's hospital is the last place you'd want to be, but also the only place you'd want to be, given the circumstances. The tiles that line the floor of the emergency wing are a lot like the blades of grass on the MCG, in that they've seen a lot over the years – heroic tales of pure courage and bravery, but also tragic stories and heartbreaking loss.

It's nice to know that so many people are carrying on Dunlop's good work in so many ways, putting all their energy into caring for those who are seriously ill and injured. Whether they're Bulldogs staff or hospital staff is irrelevant – they are cut from the same cloth. It's a credit to them that they can still find time to care for a relatively insignificant hamstring.

21 May 2009

MEETING THE MOB'S WITHERING GAZE

This week's column may be the last to leak from the pen of R. D. Murphy. I fear I may soon be chased into hiding – or, worse, disappear forever. For I am about to uncover a group so feared that until today it has remained nameless, even to a degree faceless. I speak of the football mafia.

The football mafia is the hierarchy of former great players from great teams, who proved themselves time and time again, who excelled in games where the temperature rose to epic proportions, and who now cast a watchful eye over the next generation, passing judgement on which teams and individuals are worthy and which are not.

By now you will be forming your own thoughts of who I'm talking about. My only advice is to think long and hard before pointing the finger, because there are more than a few football personalities posing as men with mob connections, when in reality they are simply not in their league. I know what I'm on about here – I've seen *The Sopranos*.

I'm speculating, but my best guess is that you only gain entry to the football 'mob' once your career has ended and, having been watched by the mafiosi throughout your career, you are given the golden handshake or some sort of secret signal of acceptance. From there, a seat is reserved for you at the table of football greatness.

Only those lucky enough to be welcomed to the group know who these mafia bosses are. But I've been doing some private eye work, and have found they have taken up some very important posts in the football world. Just like any secret society, they have infiltrated the very highest positions of power in the AFL, its clubs and the media.

Having spent last Friday night doing the media rounds before the game, I glanced along the radio press boxes and, as I expected, they were littered with men who, I believe, are big players in the underworld of the football mafia. As a true outsider to the mob myself, I studied the faces and body language of these bosses to see if there was a secret language that could be decoded, but alas, these imposing figures have been in the business of secrecy far longer than I've been trying to uncover them.

Friday night's pre-game interviews were a pretty standard affair, with the usual questions and answers. It was the subtext that caught my attention, though, and gave a brief glimpse of what the mafia might discuss behind closed doors, away from pests like me. There was, in my opinion, a definite undertone of doubt hanging over my Bulldogs.

I could see right into the eyes of some of these 'dons'. Clearly, they were reserving seats in their company for the men from this mighty team from Geelong, once they have hung up their boots. For my Bulldogs, meanwhile, there was a general look of doubt and cynicism.

I'll come back to the game itself shortly, but first I'd like to take you back to another time, another face-to-face meeting with the mob. An angry mob. It was the Monday or Tuesday night after the first final of 2008, and with our Bulldogs soundly beaten by eventual premier Hawthorn, a few teammates and I went along to a function run by the AFL Players Association to recognise the league's most valuable player.

To be frank, we felt like being anywhere else, as our performance had been quite embarrassing. Our season, which had burned brightly with promise for most of the year, was now one game away from being another disappointment.

As we arrived, we kept close and our eyes remained low. With each glance up it became obvious that the entire who's who of the football world was in attendance. It was here I got my first glimpse of the football mafia.

Fitting with the Hollywood stereotype of mafia bosses in suits, these men carried a presence in the room that no one talked about but everyone knew was there. By now my teammates and I had been separated in the crowd, and I was left feeling alone and vulnerable, like a baby panda disconnected from the safety of numbers.

As I desperately tried to find my table, I bumped straight into a man who I knew was very high up in the mob, and may even have been a don. He asked me about the game and my own form, but again it was in the subtext that I could hear him saying, 'You and your team are weak and unworthy.'

Shaken, I spun on my heels to get out of there, but could feel several other sets of eyes on me. I now know they belonged to other mafia bosses, all of them keen for their chance to say the same thing.

Friday night's game was a classic, and while clearly the mafia are still undecided on my Bulldogs, they must at least have acknowledged that the performance was worthy of their respect. But we know only too well that only repeated showings of an even greater quality – with the whole football world watching – will earn us a seat at the big table.

28 May 2009

RIGHT AS RAIN

'The best thing one can do when it's raining is to let it rain.' I've no idea who Henry Wadsworth Longfellow was, but something tells me that he'd be my kind of guy.

I've had a long love affair with rain, and the past few years of drought have been a hardship. Clearly, there are people who need the rain more than I do, but the fact remains that without the regular companion of precipitation, I just don't feel myself.

The past month or so has seen our fair city in a stunning light. As the leaves on our trees made their yearly transition from green to the lovely tangerine shades, the football season too appeared to mature before us. Football is still quintessentially a winter sport; the oval ball looks more at home on a slippery surface at the MCG. As the calendar hits winter, people do one of two things: head inside, or head to the footy. Hard to believe that, long ago, football was merely a vehicle to keep the cricketers fit over winter.

I've always thought of Melbourne as a winter city. With each tiny drop of rain it reveals another speck of soulful beauty. These downpours have been so few and far between that I almost forgot what it was like to be woken in the middle of the night by a heavy shower on my roof.

I had a birthday this week, and when I awoke to the raindrops pounding on my window I smiled to myself and enjoyed the moment. No presents required for me today – the rain was thanks enough.

Football in the wet used to be like football and liniment – one and the same. But over the past decade, playing and training in the rain have become rare delights, almost to the point of novelty.

I watched a young Demon by the name of Jack Watts play his first game on Monday, and, as we know, it was teeming. The people who know football say young Jack will play many a game for his Demons, but I wonder how many he'll play in the rain. With such a brilliantly colonial name, Watts must have wet-weather football in his blood. But with us stuffing up the planet and all that, he may not need to break out the long stops too often.

When I was younger – much younger than Watts is now – I thought it rained every night, as if they were the rules handed down by whomever was in charge. At night, Dad would tuck me in and read me a chapter from Roald Dahl, I'd drift off to sleep and wake up to see our back garden and green hills drenched. I'm sure there were times this didn't happen, but I just can't remember them.

I suppose it says as much about where I was born and brought up as it does about my slightly wonky view of the weather. I was born in Ballarat and raised in Warragul, so rain was just a part of everyday life, it seemed. Throw in my Irish heritage and it's pretty clear I never had a chance of getting the suntan I so desperately craved.

Birthdays are a funny old thing. I don't particularly like mine, but it's not like I despise it either. Some years the number just doesn't feel right. To be honest, 27 feels a little high.

If I were a rock 'n' roller, it would be a year of caution. Hendrix, Joplin, Cobain, Jones, Morrison – all heroes who fell at this particular numerical hurdle. Lucky for me I'm only a rock 'n' roll try-hard.

In football, 27 is like your 50th in regular years – you can see the end, but there's still enough time for a few more adventures. Like this weekend, when my Bulldogs and I leave this gloriously drenched city for Darwin, a place that enjoys more rainfall each year than all the other capitals in this country combined. I doubt there will be much up there on Saturday night, but I won't mind if there is.

The past few weeks I've had a bit more time on my hands to think about the rain and how Melbourne wears it so well. Too much time, really. The injury list is never where you want to be as an athlete, but, like the rain and the liniment, it's just a part of the caper.

Time off the field gave me a chance to look for a new winter coat, or, in my case, a new old winter coat. I found my precious garment in a vintage shop, in the style of what a lumberjack might wear. I imagine it was previously loved by a working man. Maybe he was a bit rough around the edges, perhaps he even had a beard. I've never met a man with a beard who I didn't like.

The forecast has been kind enough to let me wear my new lumberjack's coat most days of late, but still I haven't felt whole. My favourite jacket of all has been hanging in the closet. It's red and blue with a bit of white on it. There's a big bulldog on the front, and all my mates have one as well.

I only know it's mine because it's got a number two on the back. And on Saturday night I'll get to wear it with pride once again. Bring on the rain.

11 June 2009

A RIVAL IN
THE HOUSE

Well, folks, the lid is off. I've fought to keep it on for many weeks now, so as not to get ahead of myself and count the silverware before it hatches (or whatever silverware does), but even I know you can't argue with good form.

I'm sure many will want to take potshots at me and bring me down a peg or two, perhaps saying that I've put the cart before the horse. Or, in this case, the cart before the dog.

Maybe I should explain. I reached a stage in my life where I felt the need to invest money in a dishlicker. I never saw myself as a greyhound owner, but I've found that we're a surprisingly good fit. About a year and a half ago, my brother-in-law Dave and a couple of his mates were looking for investors for a pup. Wisely, they asked me if any of my teammates would be interested. I thought the offer might fall on deaf ears, but I had barely finished asking the question when three boys stuck their hands up high and straight and barked: 'We're in!'

So Tom Williams, Shaun Higgins, Farren Ray and I have become a dog team within a Dogs team. (Well, not really in Farren's case, but at least he gets to cling to a little of his inner Dog.) And, slowly but surely, our little pup has developed into possibly the greatest greyhound in history. Not that we'd ever get ahead of ourselves.

Coming up with a name was quite tricky, as was keeping it a secret from my long-standing four-legged friend, Arthur, who I feared would be broken-hearted if he found out I was cheating on him. We eventually settled on Ballistic Shiraz.

After waiting patiently for 18 months, our syndicate was almost as eager as the dog herself. Her first trial confirmed what we had suspected all along: she cantered home. We had a potential Hall of Famer.

Next up was her first race – with odds and everything! Our darling Ballistic Shiraz was sent out the short-priced favourite, and although she got off to her customary lightning start, she ran straight up the backside of another dog – enough to rattle any canine. No doubt she was embarrassed, but gallantly put her head down and fought on for third. We all knew she'd shown enough promise and we'd soon be rewarded.

The following week we changed Ms Shiraz's approach and lightened her training. We focused on recovery and some cross-training. It proved a masterstroke, because our princess led the whole way and crossed the line almost turned side-on, a la Usain Bolt.

That was when the syndicate took the lid off. Nothing could take the gloss off the victory, and I was positively beaming with pride. Until fate stepped in.

In my euphoric state I'd taken my winning TAB ticket

and stuck it on the fridge for all to see. The rare air of success had dulled my capacity to think clearly, because I'd forgotten about Arthur.

For a while now I've suspected that Arthur has been honing his literary skills – I often come home early from training and find him curled up reading a bit of John Harms or Tagger; the mere mention of Martin Flanagan sends him into a tail-wagging frenzy. Anyway, my worst fears were confirmed when I walked in one day last week to the sight of Arthur staring up at the fridge with tears in his eyes. The wording stood out like dog's . . . um, well, you know.

BALLISTIC SHIRAZ, $10 WIN.

Now I was the one who felt like a dog. There was no big fight, no barking or whining. It was much worse than that. For days Arthur sulked around, refusing to make eye contact, eat his food or sit on my lap. I'd never seen a dog with a broken heart before, but I knew I was witnessing one up close.

I tried to win Arthur over by taking him out of the house, giving him some fresh air, hoping to show him where my heart really lies. It proved a good move – the Community Cup at Elsternwick Park last Sunday was just how you'd imagine doggy heaven to be.

For every dog there was a flying ball or frisbee. With the football and some rock 'n' roll as the backdrop, Arthur frolicked around and let his worries wash away. After he ran himself ragged, I was a bit teary as he returned for a little rest on my lap. His spot.

I'm happy to report things are back as we both like them, and I'm yet to cash in my winning ticket for my scarlet woman.

It just doesn't feel like the right time. But I know she will race again soon, and I don't know if I'm strong enough to resist having another flutter. Man's best friend? You bet.

25 June 2009

STEP BACK AND SMELL THE ROSES

I really enjoy this time of year – and not just because of the rain, which I have a bit of a thing for. In fact, this week shapes as a sort of spring in football terms.

Spring is all about rejuvenation. It's about new life, shedding the old skin to reveal a younger version of the species. The football world this week takes its eye off the big ball for a few brief moments to study the national under-18 championships, analysing the best young kids in the land to decipher whether they are up to the rigours of the oval-balled game.

Granted, seeing these young men begin their football trade can make current players like me feel a little long in the tooth. (These boys were born in the '90s, for crying out loud!) But their very presence, the look of pure excitement in their eyes, can warm the coldest of hearts.

I read a book recently called *The Last Lecture*, written by a university professor, Randy Pausch, who was told that his body was riddled with tumours. In a bid to make sense of the news that he would soon be dead, and hoping to leave a legacy for his young family, he decided to give what is called a last lecture, in which an academic maps out his or her life lessons – a sort of 'what it's all about' presentation.

At the risk of being a bit pompous, I thought I'd have a go at what my 'last football lecture' might be. Unlike Randy Pausch, I'm not gravely ill. But with the global financial crisis upon us (and my most recent column about a greyhound), I could soon find myself on the journalistic scrapheap, so there is a parallel of sorts.

Sitting down to actually come up with what you think life – albeit a football life – is all about is more difficult than you might think. In fact, I encourage everyone to have a go at it. Good for the soul and all that. After quite a bit of time looking at a blank page and wondering what I'd say to a young punk born in the '90s, I thought I'd take a bit of advice recently given to me by a friend: 'Fake it til you make it.' I love this little pearl.

I began by scouring the web in search of some inspiration, and before long came across an Andrew Denton interview with Jerry Seinfeld on *Enough Rope*. The story goes that Jerry had to give a speech at his old high school, and was asked his three rules of life – his own last lecture. I found his response fascinating, and very relevant for a young footballer about to take his first tentative steps in the big time.

Rule 1: Work your ass off. 'Only good can come from it,' says Seinfeld. It's not hard to draw a line between this piece of advice and the football field. Not a single elite player in the AFL lacks this ethos. Clearly, there are different degrees and forms of how this work ethic is shown, but as a general rule it is a blanket over the best players going around. In coach speak, it's a 'non-negotiable'.

Rule 2: Pay attention. Seinfeld talks about really taking notice of your surroundings, absorbing the knowledge and experience of those around you. In a football sense, many of these youngsters playing for their states this week will soon be at an AFL club. The more they can absorb in a short space of time, the better off they will be. Football clubs are rich – not always in a monetary sense, but certainly in tradition and storytellers. Ask questions, and get right inside the place you'll hopefully call home for ten years or more.

Rule 3: Fall in love. Seinfeld stresses that this love need not be a romantic one (though that can't hurt either). It is more a love of the things you might miss out on if you don't adhere to Rule 2. Seinfeld makes a point of stopping and appreciating seemingly insignificant things, like a good cup of coffee. Pause to enjoy the moment. Footballers are all guilty at some stage of missing these little gems along the way.

My advice to the punks is: it will be gone much quicker than you think, so draw breath every now and then and just be in the moment, whether it's walking up the race of the MCG with the sound of the crowd shaking the walls around you, or picking up a waterlogged football from time to time to smell its familiar scent. These are tiny moments of love that will one day be lost, so take the time to appreciate them.

Seinfeld has much to offer, and not just in the business of laughs. All I would care to add for the next generation of footballers is to give black boots a go, and maybe lay off the hair dye and gel.

2 July 2009

FOOTBALL NUMEROLOGY

Let me take you back. It's a drizzly Wednesday night in Warragul. It's April 1992, about 5 pm. My very first night of football training.

This day has been circled on the calendar for weeks, maybe months, and I've been too excited at school to utter a word all day. Like all the other kids who walk from school to training, I am excited about kicking and marking and sliding around in the mud. But there is something else, something bigger.

Not that I'd utter a word, scared that if I mention it, panic will surely set in. Like a soldier in hiding, I don't dare give away my position.

Looking back, I don't know how we all knew (a few of us had older brothers, which might explain it), but we did. The first night of football training wouldn't just be about balls, witch's hats and whistles; the coach would also unload a big suitcase from his car. A suitcase full of jumpers.

No doubt there would be a time for team and selflessness during the coming season, but on this night it was every nine-year-old for himself. As each drill finished, everyone had one eye on the coach and one eye on the big suitcase sitting at the base of an old oak tree. Miss the signal and your dreams of owning a number five (Ablett) or a number three (Lyon) could evaporate.

When our coach finally relented and opened up the suitcase of tattered jumpers, it was like a scene from the movie *Platoon*: bodies flying everywhere. Somehow, I managed to sneak my arm under the pack and retrieve my jumper. It was number seven – or, as I would have said at the time, 'a Winmar'.

I've never been into numbers, but football jumper numbers are different, it seems. They mean more. Last week, my team-mates and I got a nice little surprise from our adult football club. After finishing our trackwork, we returned to the sanctuary that is the change rooms. These rooms are pretty straightforward, made up of 40 or so lockers. Until now they had just been a place to keep the tools of our trade, but suddenly they had become something much more.

On the front of each locker door now is history, a Bulldog lineage, if you like. Coming in from training, we were each greeted by a locker door boasting the freshly painted names of men who had worn our jumper in 100 or more games for our club.

And there was more. There were other names painted in a gold tint, reserved for the legends who had played in our one and only premiership in 1954.

When you break it down, the number you wear on your back is little more than a way of identifying each player on the ground. But like many things in football, these small things carry a deeper meaning, a link to the history of an ancient tribe.

I sometimes get the feeling that the world sees young people these days as less sentimental beings. I don't think I've ever had this conversation with anyone – nor have I had this accusation levelled at me – it's just a gut instinct. And I don't think it's accurate.

Now, more than ever, we live in a world that is fast – too fast, perhaps – and this idea of 'permanent' or 'forever' is becoming less common. The world's advances in technology have set a pace that leaves many reeling. It is, of course, the younger generations who use this technology more than any others, but it is a world and ethos we've been thrust into. We don't know any different.

I've been thinking about my generation of footballers, a mere snippet of our male generation at large. And my mental wanderings have led me to ponder the increasing number of tattoos seen on players' arms.

I think the symbolism goes a lot deeper than trying to be 'trendy'. I believe it is the result of a generation being denied the security of 'forever'. Life is one fast-food chain after another. We are smack-bang in the middle of the Twitter age, where communication is quick and often frivolous.

Often the body art of my generation has a significance not dissimilar to that of our new football lockers. Tattoos are of a tribal nature, a family coat of arms, or a memorial for a loved one who has passed on. We have no real feel for something permanent, so we have inked our bodies to get something deeper, more lasting. I might be way off – maybe the kids just want to look like Becks – but I really hope I'm not.

My point is that I believe the youth of today are very sentimental. You only had to see the faces of the players as we studied our lockers last week, reading the names of those who had played for the club with such honour and distinction. It gave all of us the tingles.

I've heard Terry Wheeler speak to the playing group before, about us being custodians of the jumper at the moment. That responsibility will be passed on again. Quite simply, it is our job to do our best while we have it.

Our brand-new changerooms are starting to get that lovely lived-in look and smell. The names on the lockers have lifted the room to another level, and other things will be added over the coming months and years to make it our own.

All of it will come together, with the sweat and liniment in the air, to give the rooms that wholesome, football club feel. And my teammates and I know how privileged we are to call it home.

9 July 2009

FATHER, SONS AND FAMILIES

*'It is not flesh and blood but the heart
which makes us fathers and sons.'*
JOHANN SCHILLER

Eight posts, a big patch of grass and an oddly shaped red ball
make up the game of Aussie rules at its most basic level, but
we are all well aware that the significance it brings to people's
lives runs deep. If the game were just about kicks, marks and
handballs, I'm sure it would have perished by now.

Something that has come into sharp focus this past week
is the notion of football and family, and in particular the bond
between a father and son. Not to ignore the role of women in
football or family for one second, but I've been trying to delve
a bit deeper into this special relationship that fathers and sons
have with our game.

Some of my most vivid early memories of my dad involve
football in some shape or form, and having a son of my own
these days makes these special times come flooding back. They
are memories that stay with us forever.

Going to Waverley as a little boy, pelting down with rain
and only five degrees, eating a jam doughnut with only my

jacket and Dad's arm around me for warmth. When I think about that day now, I wonder if those little memories are what makes us who we are.

Growing up in my family, football was always just there. It would thrill us, it was the source of fights and all sorts of arguments, but ultimately it became part of the stitching that bound us as a family.

Being drafted to a league club is very exciting and full of enormous challenges, but one thing that has snuck up on me over the years is this notion of family, and what it means to be part of one as big as a football club. While you don't share the same family tree or surname, the dynamic is similar to the one you had with those who grew up under your roof.

Football clubs are made up of many different personalities, but so often it seems that all you need is one thing in common. Just like a family around the kitchen table, arguing and laughing, the same goes for the atmosphere within a club. There's an enormous amount of laughter and goodwill, but also times of tension, frustration and hostility. Nothing is held back in either 'family'. All the cards are on the table, and you see each other for exactly who and what you are.

This idea of fathers and their sons can take on different forms, as the earlier quote from Mr Schiller suggests. In a football sense, the term 'father figure' is a well-worn one to describe all manner of mentors. They all have something in common with our real fathers – for some reason, some people just offer others shelter from a storm. As a young man coming into a football club, you soon find yourself gravitating towards men who provide such shelter.

In my draft year of 1999, I was lucky to walk nervously into a club that was full of men who offered shelter for me and my rookie mates. Luke Darcy, Todd Curley, Matthew Croft, Scott Wynd, Chris Grant, Steve Kretiuk, Simon Garlick, Scott West, Rohan Smith, Brad Johnson – all men whose wings we knew we could climb under when it felt too cold and miserable to plough on alone.

Over time, Gia, Shaggy, Mitch, Gilb and I would find something in one, two or three of those players that went beyond just a footy teammate or friend. This deeper connection with certain people is one of the great things about life, and not just at a footy club. Although I'm sure we didn't realise it at the time, pretty soon your footy club becomes like an extension of the family you threw broccoli at across your kitchen table.

As the years pass, it's funny how much of a peek you get inside the lives of your teammates and their families. With each passing season, their parents and siblings become almost a further extension of this ever-growing family. You become very familiar with your teammates' fathers, in particular. I don't know exactly why this is, but at a guess, we blokes simply associate the relationship of father and son immediately with football.

In the rooms after games or at club functions, you see on dads' faces a special look of pride. It's not boastful, but a look of pure joy at seeing their boys live their dreams. We lost a member of the Bulldogs' extended family last week, meaning this notion of fathers and sons has hit home to one of our own in the worst possible way.

Being a good mate of Lindsay Gilbee, I naturally got to know his dad, Lawrie, as well. I didn't know him well, but certainly enough to see that he was a person of the highest quality. And I saw that look of joyous pride on his face whenever he was around his son, and his own extended family of the red, white and blue.

Today, our Bulldog family gathers around one of its own to say goodbye. We'll be thinking of Gilb and his family. And I'll be thinking of another famous family quote: 'What greater thing is there for two human souls, than to feel that they are joined for life . . . to be one with each other in silent, unspeakable memories?'

6 August 2009

TIME TO SORT THE WHEAT FROM THE CHAFF

'Twas a very confusing and somewhat upsetting week for me, folks, and it all started before a ball was even bounced. News had started filtering through via this weird thing they call the web on Saturday morning. Apparently a fight had broken out between two of our most treasured working-class heroes, Noel and Liam Gallagher of Oasis fame.

When I got to the Dome on Sunday for the match against the Magpies, I was well and truly dishevelled by the bust-up of this pioneering Britpop band. Search as I did my soul for answers, none were forthcoming.

I made my way around the rooms to ask my Bulldogs team-mates if they thought we should wear black armbands to commemorate the tragic events, and their responses were similar to that of Jarvis's mum when I had told her the day before. 'Um . . . Bob, you've got issues.'

So I bundled up my grief and put the matter aside; best to win the game of footy first, I thought, and then mark the day by singing 'Wonderwall' instead of our more traditional 'Sons of the West'.

It had been a pretty ordinary couple of days up to this point, and then, with only minutes left to tick by before we were to run out against Collingwood, it became apparent that the People's Beard would be a late withdrawal from his 100th game! (Not to get too technical here, but while it was indeed supposed to be Ben Hudson's 100th, it will in fact be only game number 87 for the People's Beard.)

AFL footy is all about mental strength, so despite these two events potentially disrupting my preparation, I dug deep, went out there and got the job done for the red, white and blue.

Just on the game, I'm not sure if I've ever played in a more complex last quarter before in my life. At times I felt as if there were three games of football going on – the first was us trying to get through the Collingwood spare players in defence (like a miniature game of chess); the second was the result for the four points; and the third facet of the big picture was the ladder positioning.

People keep asking about finishing third or fourth, and who you want to play in the first week of the finals. For me, it was less about who we wanted to play than just wanting to get a place higher. Footballers don't tend to overthink things. See ball, chase ball, and keep doing so until the big whistle sounds.

That's enough serious talk in this column for one week. Now, if I may turn your attention to the changing seasons. Winter into spring has something special about it, and the smell of jasmine hitting the nostrils to mark the occasion should give us all a little pep up and a fresh start.

Speaking of fresh starts, I thought this week was a great opportunity to cut away the fat of the home-and-away season and have us looking a little sharper for the finals. Ladies and gentleman, welcome to our first ever 'Footy Garage Sale'! Yes, a chance to sift through the garage that's cluttered with all the bits and bobs that make up our game, and choose what stays and what is to be chucked.

The format is not important, but I'll get the ball rolling with a short list of 'Get Rid Ofs' and 'Keeps'. From there, I imagine it will take off and get the good people arguing the case for and against their own bits of footy junk. Yes, it'll have the punters arguing the toss even more than Thingamajiggy's Top 50 Players.

BOB MURPHY'S GARAGE SALE

Get Rid of . . .

- White boots (I don't get it)
- Hair dye on players (it's an epidemic)
- Spiritual tatts (what's wrong with spider webs on your elbows?)
- Football red-carpet specials (in fact, any football personality in the social pages)
- Players faking a fall when someone pushes them in a bid to have the free kick reversed.
- Celebrity tipping (like Oasis splitting up, apparently no one cares)
- Solariums (it's winter, come on)
- Processes (all of them, no exceptions)
- Americanisms (Kick it from the paint? Come on, Dwayne!)

Keep . . .

- Property stewards (heart and soul)
- The little league (bless 'em)
- Ground invasions (it's a matter of national pride)
- Liniment (if you could bottle football as cologne, this would be it)
- *Before the Game* (the players' football show of choice)
- Farewell games (they show the game can have a heart, even in a world of accountants)
- Club songs (granted, a few of the interstate ones need some work, but overall they're brilliant)
- Beards (Huddo has shown the way; disciples welcome)
- Warm-up laps (clear the head)
- Brett Kirk's hair (Oasis quality)

3 September 2009

ACTIONS SPEAK LOUDER THAN WORDS ON PRELIMINARY FINAL DAY

Walking is good for the soul, they say, so with that in mind, last week I put Arthur on the lead, put my iPod in and took a stroll around my neck of the woods . . .

Um, you know what? I can't be arsed this week. Every week in this column I try to bend things that have little or no significance and apply them to the football landscape. If I'm a few words short, I throw in my silly little elongated dog, maybe Jarvis and his mum, or even a gratuitous mention of the People's Beard. But this week is different.

Now, it's true that I did take a walk and listen to some music one day last week, and quite a few anecdotes came out of that little trip that were potentially relevant to football and this column. But I don't feel this week needs any euphemisms, quotes, double entendres or even canine trickery to gloss it up. This is a week that needs no varnish at all. Preliminary Final weekend is exactly what it's always been: football heaven.

Melbourne at the moment feels how I imagine Rome would have in the Colosseum's heyday. They say all roads lead to Rome – well, for the last two weeks and the next two, all roads lead to Melbourne, and specifically to the MCG.

There is a different feel to finals football, no doubt. More people converge on the games; there is obviously more at stake and a bigger effort required. But it's the silences that I've noticed more than anything else. The eerie hum of 80,000 people standing in silence before the national anthem is just as spine-tingling as the roar of the crowd when the anthem stops.

This week at the Kennel a big crowd turned out to see their Doggies have a run – probably the biggest gathering I've seen attend training. Add to that the sun shining and the stillness of the air, and it certainly felt different to what we're used to. I presume our supporters whooped and hollered in the outer last Friday night to show their support. But to be honest, it was again the silence that struck me more than the noise.

As we warmed up and went about our skill work, there was naturally voice, instruction, encouragement. But it was the eye contact made in brief glimpses that stays with me. Some teammates I've known and played alongside for the best part of a decade, others only for a year or two, but when eyes meet in silence and you both acknowledge the anticipation of what's ahead, it is something pretty special. Maybe it's these moments that draw us to team sport.

So, with the world seemingly converging on our fair city this week, you would think that the life of a footballer would become hectic, certainly noisier, and maybe even a little rushed. But I've found the exact opposite. While a hurricane appears to be whipping up around each of the four teams left, from within (and I'm assuming it's the same for the Saints, Cats and Magpies) there is a calmness. The eye of the storm, if you will.

Of course, we're all aware of the interest and buzz around town among football followers over what's up for grabs, but those we see everyday – teammates, club officials, friends and family – seem to huddle around one another and keep the swirling winds at bay.

Well, the family are a bit chirpy – they need tickets, after all – but again it feels quieter than normal. Even as I sit here jotting down my thoughts, the house feels quiet, the sort of quiet that softens a home when a new baby is brought into the world.

Four teams lay it all on the line this weekend for a spot in the big dance. Hundreds of kicks, marks and handballs will carry a significance of their own, deciding which two teams will come out on top. But for me it will be the few poignant moments of silence before, during and after the battle that will tell me whether the angels shall carry the Bulldogs to the grandest stage of all.

17 September 2009

2010

ALL CH-CH-CHANGE WHEN AGE KEEPS YOU ON YOUR TOES

My toenails have aged. Ch-ch-changes are constant and infinite, some good and some bad, but they're a big part of what makes the world go round. Our challenge is to roll with the punches.

But this changing (or, rather, ageing) of my toenails has really got me flummoxed. I'm aware it's not the most desirable of topics to open up this first column of the year with, but if it's affecting me, then chances are a few of you are equally bewildered by the state of your own toenails.

Perhaps when David Bowie sang 'turn and face the strain' in his epic 'Changes' he'd just taken a look at his big toenail, all hardened, thickened and threatening. Or perhaps not. (I'd set myself a target of avoiding referencing song lyrics this year, and have lasted one whole sentence. Oh well.)

But I'm interested in what else has changed of late. Our little family has moved out to the burbs since I last penned a line in *The Age*; add to that the addition of our baby girl to the clan and you could say our little world has been rocked by change. We wouldn't have it any other way.

The move was somewhat reluctant. My wife and I have adored the inner-city living style for most of the noughties, but Jarvis has had a big pre-season, bulked up a treat and needs some space to stretch his wings. Out here the air is clean, the people are cheery and there is virtually no sign of crime or social decay. Still, I'm sure we'll grow to love it.

This revelation about the toenails came only last week as I sat with Arthur – my elongated dog who hates wet ground – on the back porch and went about trimming my toenails. I'm not sure if that's just what happens to toenails when you're a shade under 28, or if a life spent crammed into football boots, there to be kicked, twisted and stood on, accelerates the ageing process and gives them such a ghastly, hard exterior.

It doesn't really matter, I guess. Some things just make you feel old when you're not quite ready for them. I don't mind, for instance, the grey hair that comes through more frequently with each haircut. It's gradual. It lets you know you're ageing with class and dignity.

Gee, it's nice to have the footy back. If Melbourne were a person it would cast a solemn figure in the summertime, trudging along the sidewalk, sweaty and inadequately dressed, wearing a forlorn expression and the posture of someone who has just lost $50.

Our Melbourne person is neither man nor woman, just a being that craves the change of seasons and the return of the oval ball. Our fair city is at its most serene as the mercury drops and the masses rise to see their teams play on the big stage. As the leaves make their annual, gorgeous change, our Melbourne hits its stride and thrusts it shoulders back, and suddenly the clothes that hung so awkwardly on its frame fit snugly, complementing the different shades.

I'm clearly gushing a bit over old Melbourne town, which I think must have something to do with my latest love affair – train travel. I can't believe it's taken me this long, to be honest. All these years sat in my car, crawling through the traffic. I had no idea I could be riding the rails, reading my book and getting under the skin of this city I thought I knew so well.

Falling in love with train travel has been the silver lining of our change of address. It's a fair hike to training from my ranch now, and I must admit I feared my old XP, Jok (aka Frankie), might not cope with the workload. But to my pleasant surprise, catching the train has added a certain romance to my week that driving just didn't have. Jok is happy about it, too, I reckon. His weekdays are freed up to enjoy the fresh air now, saving himself for the heavy training load of Sunday drives.

The train is a bit of a hit with my little sidekick, Jarvis, too. Twice a week J commutes with his dad to the new childcare facility at the Whitten Oval. He loves his trains almost as much as he loves his Bulldogs. Some of you might even see us – we'll be the ones struggling to carry our bags and racing to make our train. Do say hello.

Speaking of the Bulldogs, it's been a pretty big month out in the west, to be sure. But I think we've managed to fly under the radar so far in 2010, and even kept our new recruit Barry Hall virtually hidden from prying eyes.

Seriously, it was a wonderful thing to win the NAB Cup two weeks ago. The red, white and blue army has waited a long time to see a trophy of any kind. Along with about 40,000 other

Bulldog fanatics, I thoroughly enjoyed watching the big boy in number 28 kick a few, too. Barry has given himself wholly to our club, and we have welcomed him with open arms. But we'll need Barry and 21 other Bulldogs at or near their best to beat Collingwood on Sunday.

And so it begins again. Plenty of ch-ch-changes, shocks and surprises are in store in the months ahead, I know that much. And I know footy is back. All aboard!

25 March 2010

COMING TO GRIPS WITH A SHAKY PRE-GAME TRADITION

'Why don't you get off the fence with all this fluffy stuff and have a crack for once?'

The gym of a football club pretty much works like a court of law – or it does out at the Kennel, anyway. Any number of accusations can and will be levelled at anyone, anytime, if the mood should strike. Last week, as we prepared for Round 1, it was my turn. As I went about my weights training, I was set upon by some Bulldog barristers about this little column I write for *The Age*.

It started innocently enough, when Ben Hudson (aka the People's Beard) asked me what I had in store for column number one of 2010. Fair question, I thought. Ben is getting a little tired of his beard being name-checked pretty much every week in these pages (oh dear, I've done it again), so I guess he was within his rights to wonder how the season in print would kick off.

I gave the Beard a vague answer about toenails, train rides, David Bowie lyrics and the like, and the mood changed quicker than Will Minson's mind. My feisty Italian friend Daniel Giansiracusa joined Huddo, creating a two-on-one.

This is pretty much how the judicial system of the gym works at our footy club. The accusation is levelled, the murmuring crowd gathers, and finally the accused is backed into a corner, frantically defending his honour against an angry mob. Years of experience have taught me it's a lot more fun being part of the angry mob.

So, with the overwhelming view of my peers in mind, I think it's time to add my voice to an issue that's been bubbling along in the AFL for some time now. An issue that isn't so much a call to arms as a call to hands. Hands that shake. Yes, the great handshake debate is back on the agenda!

Readers with long memories will recall that 'the shake' rated a mention in these parts last year, too. I suppose it tickles my fancy because I've always shook hands before a game.

I'm not completely sure why this is. I know I shake hands after a game because my dear old Da preached how important that is, but he never mentioned anything about pre-game offerings of luck that I can remember. Perhaps it's because I grew up playing basketball as well as footy, and in the culture of basketball you acknowledge not just your direct opponent, but the entire opposing team.

Something I want to avoid in this whole dilemma is any hint of pomposity. None of this 'I shake my opponent's hand, so thou shalt do as I do'. I'm simply intrigued by this small but potentially iconic ritual of the game.

I first thought seriously about it when Nick Maxwell offered his hand to David Neitz a few years ago, only to have the offer rejected. Just as fascinating was Brock McLean doing the same thing to Brett Kirk before a pre-season battle this year.

In my research (another first), I found that the simple act of shaking hands has a somewhat clouded history: no one can be absolutely certain where or when it started. The etiquette of knights, maybe? British nobles? Perhaps the Romans, who were said to shake each other's forearms to check for weapons?

I doubt McLean or Neitz had any of this in mind when they refused to shake. What I can be sure of is that, in modern times, the handshake stands for one of three things: 'hello', 'goodbye' or 'we agree'.

It's this third interpretation that I'm interested in, and the very reason why I still shake hands before a game. For me, it's a gesture that says, 'We agree that, after this moment of good-will, we will do everything we can to beat each other.'

Clearly, this is not the view of everyone in football, let alone at my own club. I've had some robust discussions on the topic with some of my teammates. That's what happens with inter-pretations. But anyone who sees it as a sign of surrender or weakness should look past me and on to Brett Kirk. Surely there has never been a more respected warrior in the game.

Speaking with teammates, former players and football people in general, I've encountered a wide range of views in regard to the shake. Most told me they choose not to offer their hand, but would accept their opponent's if it was extended to them.

I don't recall ever having my hand refused before a game, but there have been some interesting reactions. My personal favourite was last year when my Collingwood opponent got a bit of a shock when I offered him the hand of goodwill. He shook it, but then immediately slammed his elbow into my back. I loved this. Goodwill was established with the shake, then the rules of battle were established immediately after with the elbow.

To the surprise of one of my teammates, this same opponent offered his hand before the game on Sunday. Perhaps it's taking off. And about time, too.

2 April 2010

---

*My Collingwood opponent that day was Harry
O'Brien (now Heritier Lumumba). The great handshake
debate is still chugging along. We must push on . . .*

TEACH YOUR CHILDREN WELL

Football is a funny little trade – and a trade is exactly how I see it. It's to be toiled at, is rarely mastered, and requires more than a few skills from left field. A job it ain't, though.

Away from the field of play and the spotlight, there are a few things that must be completed as part of this trade. I talk of school visits and footy clinics.

Friday-night football is exciting to watch, exhilarating to be a part of and absolutely disastrous if you miss out on the four points. A weekend of regret, guilt and just the right amount of anxiety ensues. We were pretty darn relieved to get away with the win on Friday night. Just as well, too, because not only were those four points against Melbourne crucial to our season, but every single Bulldogs player had an Auskick clinic the following morning.

Kids in the west are pretty tough, and they like winners. As the People's Beard and I wandered over to the crowd gathered at the home of the Newport Power, we were warmed by the inner strength of victors, and by two big, strong flat whites to go. Little kids are the bees knees, the cat's pyjamas or (as my Gen Y teammates might say) 'da bomb'. Suffice to say, the kids are all right – as long as you win.

Over the course of my football adventure, footy clinics have become a prominent part of the season. Typically, a mix of kids from all ages and supporting the whole spectrum of teams sit and stare and raise their hands to the point their shoulders strain. They want to know everything about footy. They just love the oval ball.

What is somewhat amusing is that, no matter where we go for these clinics and school visits, there is always a slight sense of deja vu. Whether we've been sent to Warragul, Colac or just down the road to Seddon, I can be almost certain that at least one of three staple questions (and sometimes all of them) will be raised by the little 'uns.

The first is a constantly evolving staple of discontent. This season it goes: 'Where is Barry Hall?' But over the years you could substitute Barry's name with Chris Grant, Libba, Brad Johnson and, more recently, Cooney and Aker. But right now Big Barry is the apple of the kids' eyes.

My job as an AFL player at these visits is to teach the kids about healthy eating, skill technique and leadership, but often my concept of a successful and worthwhile visit comes down to whether I can break the bad news to the audience gently enough: 'Even though Barry isn't here today, kids, we're going to have fun just the same with little old me!' It's a battle.

The second standard query from the little people, and one that I'm constantly bemused by in a grammatical sense, is: 'What's the hardest team you've versed?' Now, it's not for me to belittle the littlies on the grounds of grammar (my editor here at *The Age* will attest to that). But I'm bemused by the consistency of this question.

I reckon I've done well over 100 of these visits in my time, and that quirky question will have been asked every time and in that exact way. 'Versed' was never a popular word when Craig Starcevich visited my primary school in 1990, but it seems like it's gone gangbusters in the 20 years since.

The third and most adorable statement that will inevitably be said by the motley crew of whipper-snappers goes a little like this: 'My dad plays football.' Just like the first two, this statement/question is a footy clinic standard, and I've laughed out loud every time someone has thrown it into the fray. It's funny because it stops the flow of play, so to speak – and because of the flow-on effect such a confusing statement has on every mob of kids I've fronted.

Pretty soon you can't hear yourself think, and you're desperately trying to wrestle back control of the group as a sea of voices yells out things like: 'My dad builds cars!' 'My sister has a puppy dog!' 'I like purple!' Bless 'em.

The kids at Newport Power were just like every other junior footy club I've been to: a cluster of brilliant little individuals with their own take on our great game. Like me, they also appreciated the importance of having a sausage in bread after Saturday training, which certainly endeared them to the People's Beard. He'd wolfed down half a dozen before I lost count.

By Tuesday night we were at it again, this time back at the Kennel with another group of little champions. With the winter chill finally upon us, we opted for a bit of Bulldog tiggy to keep everyone warm, and big kids and little kids alike were soon racing around, chanting and carrying on like lunatics.

Then one little fella took a tumble, the tears welled up and his cries were like the air coming out of a tyre. Footballers just weren't interesting to the kids anymore – having wanted nothing more in the world one minute than an autograph, now all our little group could think of was the comfort of home.

Teams win and lose every week, and supporters' emotions zip around like yo-yos. As sick of footy as those kids were by the end of Tuesday night, they'll be bouncing out of bed again by Saturday morning, ready to embrace it again in all its glory. We can learn a lot from them, God love 'em. We all have weeks like that.

13 May 2010

OLD DOG HAS A COUPLE OF GOOD JUMPS LEFT

'I can't let you go home, Mr Murphy, until you've urinated.'

Ah, just one of the many joys of surgery. But how did we get here again? Let's backtrack a little, shall we? The Canberra road trip started well enough. I left my little family with everyone in good spirits, not least our youngest Ms Murphy. If she had any more fun jumping than she does now, I fear her little head might just fall off.

Despite my indifference to wearing tracksuits, my teammates and I trotted into Tullamarine with a point to prove. Sitting at four wins and three losses and coming up against the Swans, we needed a big effort from everyone to get over the line.

The airport was buzzing. Hawthorn great Robert DiPierdomenico swooshed past me in a rush for his plane, and I had to do a double-take on the way into the Qantas lounge as Joe Hockey dashed out. I wondered if I would come across any more pollies in our nation's capital.

As I approached the shiny glass doors, a familiar face emerged. I stood and stared, time stood still, and I shook the hand of Paul Kelly. I was struck by serendipity. This man's songs and words have almost chaptered my life. One song, 'When I First Met Your Ma', made a brief appearance at our wedding, and another, 'They Thought I Was Asleep', is our family's lullaby of choice on a long car trip. Paul Kelly sort of hangs in the air at our house. He could not possibly know this, so after shaking his hand and wishing him well, I let him go. Begrudgingly, I let him go. He must get that a lot.

I was a happy little Bulldog. As I stepped onto the escalator I could feel it lifting me skyward. He's good, that Kelly kid. I hadn't had that good a start to a road trip since I saw Tim Rogers swan through the airport in a three-piece suit and with what looked like vintage turquoise luggage. That particular trip was a rocking success, and after my brief brush with more Australian rock royalty I could see only glory on the horizon.

But of course, this knee of mine suffers from a bipolar disorder. The surgeon calls it 'jumper's knee', but that's in a medical sense. I know the soul of my knee, and it is a real moody bastard.

Preparing for the game, I went through everything I always do to help me play well, but still the concern in my gut grew as each hour passed. Something didn't feel right. I knew I was in trouble early in the game. With this knee of mine, it's not so much a matter of if there's pain, but what sort of pain.

Playing in the back half I was able to shuffle around and gather a few kicks, but thankfully the boys up the field did such a good job that I wasn't exposed, as I might have been on another day. Pushing both hands into Jude Bolton's back to help me stop and change direction sent off a little alarm in my head that all was not well in the psyche of my moody knee. A couple of minor incidents put too much pressure on the joint, and, somewhat predictably, my day was done. The blow was softened by a comfortable win and my Dogs playing some of our best football for the year.

We adjourned to the changerooms to sing our tribal hymn, and the most famous and powerful of Bulldog belles joined in on the frivolity. I would have loved to hang around and chat with Julia Gillard, our deputy PM and number one fan, but I had a date with our doctors.

They weren't smiling. A couple of scans ensued, I caught up with all my old pals at the Prahan medical centre, and even got a chance to fix up my tab with Frank the coffee man. (If there's one place you shouldn't have a bar tab, it's the hospital.) One look at the scans supported my sinking feeling of the past couple of weeks. A cyst that had been removed last October had returned and needed to be taken out arthroscopically.

Nothing shatters your ego and brings you back to earth quite like a hospital hair net and see-through cloth underpants. Actually, urinating in a plastic bottle while wearing your new underpants tops that.

With the cyst again homeless, and me medicated for the pain, all I was left with in recovery was a hint of sadness. The feeling that, perhaps, something was slipping away from me. My body and my season have stalled. Again. All it takes is a moment of inspiration, clarity or epiphany – something to snap you out of a downward spiral of self-pity. I was on the lookout for mine.

'There's more chance of me being full-forward for the Doggies than taking over from Kevin,' came the first. I could see the headline of this very column: Murphy out, Gillard in. She'd be all right, too. Lots of forward pressure.

The second moment that I hope will propel me back to business came from the youngest of Bulldog belles, Jarvis's little sister, who hadn't stopped jumping since I last saw her days ago. There was her dad, all bruised and bandaged with his 'jumper's knee', and the apple of his eye showing him how it's done. Stalled but not stopped – there's still a bit of jump left.

Suddenly, it feels like something has come charging back.

20 May 2010

OUR GREAT
AND PROUD CLUB

Saturday night was the inaugural Footscray–Western Bulldogs Hall of Fame function, and it was a beauty. Fourteen
hundred people turned out to honour the first inductees. Our
champions. But in reality, the night was about a lot more. In
effect, it was a history lesson on Footscray, football, culture
and unity.

I take my hat off to the many people who orchestrated the
night. As much as they would have planned meticulously to
create a night to remember, the mark it leaves on people so
often comes down to whether there is a bit of magic in the air.

Our newest official legend, Charlie Sutton, took care of
the magic in his sermon to the red, white and blue mass. The
best speeches I've ever heard are from people who put their
vulnerabilities on display; it's these weak points that make us
human and give the words a bit more credibility.

When Charlie arrived in a wheelchair, it knocked the wind
out of everyone. Charlie was vulnerable, no doubt about it,

but he was there because he cares. Looking frailer than we'd ever seen him, he took to the stage and spoke with a passion as big as the room itself.

'Hit 'em hard, hit 'em bloody often,' he cried.

You knew you were witnessing an iconic moment, something that would stay with you forever.

Our two legends on the night were Charlie and, of course, the great EJ Whitten. EJ's shadow looms large out in Footscray, and it made me think that with him being such a huge part of Footscray and football, we – as in Bulldogs people – have shared him with you all.

But Charlie is all ours. He is so dear to us, perhaps because he more than anyone else in our history put the team before himself. By simply being there on Saturday night, he showed he still does. When asked by the MC who his favourite current-day player was, Charlie replied that it was not about that – it was about the team. Every footy club needs a Charlie Sutton.

Along with Charlie and EJ, the tales of the other inductees evoked plenty of pride and humour. The list runs just as you would expect for a Hall of Fame – the names sparkle. Hopkins, Ware, Olliver, Hickey, Morrison – all class.

On into the club's glory years, with my number two locker forefather, Jack Collins, and gentle giant John Schultz. John spoke with the players during the week about the Bulldog heritage book, which he has been instrumental in compiling. It's a beautifully presented hardcover full of Footscray players and their stories in their own words. I'm saving a nice bottle of red to savour that one with at season's end.

And the great names rolled on: Beasley, Templeton, Dempsey, Hawkins, Liberatore and the great Chris Grant. Every player was greeted with the warmest of ovations. Champions in front of their own people, they must've been as proud as punch.

Along with the induction of greats and legends alike, the night was also about recognising pivotal moments in the club's history – not an easy job when you consider how long this football club has been around. Again, they hit the mark.

Neil Sachse's story is one of tragedy and inspiration. Playing in only his second game for the Bulldogs, he was hit awkwardly from front-on with his head down. Neil broke his back; he would never walk again, let alone play football.

They played the footage a few times and I found myself unable to look away. I leaned over to Shaun Higgins and Adam Cooney, who were at my table, and made the comment that as ghastly as the image was, we'd all seen guys take hits just as big as the one that broke Neil's back. What a price to pay.

To see Neil today is pretty bloody inspiring. Having started a foundation to raise money for spinal cord research is an amazing achievement in itself, and his recognition on the night was a masterstroke.

The '54 guys were honoured, of course, and the image of the surviving members huddled around Charlie was a classic. So too was Harvey Stevens' anecdote from the day of the Grand Final, when he was late to the game because he had worked all morning at the butcher's. He got to the MCG and the game had started. Brilliant.

The third of the pivotal moments was the fightback in 1989, led by Irene Chatfield. Our football club as we know it would quite simply not be here today if not for the hard work and determination of Irene, Peter Gordon and many others.

Backs to the wall and with the wolves snapping at their heels, it took an almighty effort from everyone involved to turn it around. A team effort. A bit like the one that's happening in this current season.

Our club motto in Latin reads *Cede Nullis*, which translates as 'yield to none'. If we've learned anything in the last week, it's that our great and proud club is more powerful than any individual. Just as Charlie reminded us, it's all about the team.

3 June 2010

RIDING THE FRIDAY NIGHT WAVE

We humans can have anywhere up to 70,000 thoughts in a single day. How many of these are pivotal? How many are poignant? How many are absurd? Before I get howled down for being a jock capable of only a few hundred thoughts in a single day, let me walk you through my day last Friday.

I've been bunkered down all morning; the outside world barely exists on game day. No papers are fetched, coffee is brewed on the stove, mobile phones are a no-no. As ever, Jarvis's mum has me pegged: 'You're difficult to be around before you play. You're a bit . . . tense.'

Apart from the generic things a footballer does before a game (stretch, drink water, eat pasta, blah blah), there is plenty going on in our heads, despite our vacant looks and two-word answers. Honest!

After lunch I look out the back window. Grey clouds hover on the horizon and showers pour down throughout the afternoon. Not drizzle, but proper rain. With each drop I'm more certain I'll be wearing my long stops tonight. A little voice whispers, 'Are your wet-weather boots worn in enough? They're not ready!' The voice is ignored and all boots are cleaned and packed in my bag.

In the car at 4.55 pm, the rain has softened. I've left about ten minutes earlier than usual, hoping to dodge Melbourne's traffic congestion. Soundtrack for the trip? A smokin' group called Those Darlins.

Really nervous now, thinking about the game and what is at stake, and my hand taps the steering wheel all the way to the 'G. I soon regret leaving early – it's only 5.10 as I round the corner to the ground. The game will start at 7.40. Only a few staff mill around the rooms, so I pick up a football and wander out onto the majestic green lady.

The MCG is very special, but last Friday she looked even more beautiful than usual. With the lights only half lit, the hallowed turf glowed emerald green, and above me was pitch-black sky. The rain had moved on, offering hope that what might have been a mud wrestle could still scale heights befitting the stage.

Boots are laid out for inspection. I stick with the long-stopped variety – the little voice I can handle, but coach Rodney Eade's bigger voice asking, 'Why did you slip over all night?' I can't bear to comprehend.

Boots, shorts and warm-up kit on, I spend the next ten minutes trotting around, obsessing about the tightness of my boots. Lucky I did leave early; these boots have chewed up a lot of time.

Team meeting time. We all seem to sit in the same spots, I notice, and I take mine on the floor down front. On the magnetic board my name sits next to Shaun Burgoyne's, and all over the ground are the one-on-one battles football people love to see. Players get excited by this, too; we judge ourselves on our ability to win one-on-one.

Running up the race, anxiety disappears and I'm immersed in my favourite pre-game time the few moments of silence before we emerge as a team onto the ground. A holy and fragile thing is team spirit, and those few silent seconds heading up the race are pretty special, just me and my teammates. I think to myself how much I'll miss those precious seconds one day.

We run out, and the banner has plenty on it; I don't catch it all, but the last line is 'Well done, Julia'. I can join the dots on that one.

The game is ferocious. Individual battles are waged all over the ground, but even as a player I can tell the crowd is enthralled by one in particular. The Buddy and Brian show is in full swing, and won't let up for the whole night.

The ball is flying around and it feels like a final. It even looks like a final, and there are stars everywhere. Beau Muston seems to be lost and is following me around when surely he should be following Gilbee or Hargrave. A mini game of human chess ensues. He seems to want to push and shove; I consider doing likewise, then remember I am a beanpole.

Best to get on the move. I drag Muston to where I think the ball will end up (usually Buddy and Brian), so he plays as a forward and tries to get it. We switch spots and I defend him, hoping to outpoint him and win the ball. It's hard to say, let alone execute.

At one point I grimace. Muston spots it, and cheekily asks how my knee is. I love the way he goes about it – a totally selfless player who appreciates the humour in irony; my knee pains must pale in comparison to the three reconstructions he's endured. We march on.

The game doesn't let up; my hands will be shaking long after the siren goes, but during the match my thoughts shoot out like shrapnel from a grenade. The last few minutes are like a streetfight, and when all is on the line the Hawks land the better punches. Hodge and Mitchell twist the blade. The siren sounds, and the majestic lady swallows us up.

As good a game as it was, only Hawthorn people are smiling. Footscray folk are shattered; it scarcely needs mentioning that we players are Footscray people too.

The soundtrack on the car ride home is one of silence. My hands still tap the steering wheel, but it is only the last of the adrenaline working its way out of my body. I heard someone say this week that football is about memories and regrets. It's no wonder we have trouble getting to sleep.

8 July 2010

A CLUB STANDS AS ONE

Footy can feel like it's all about lines. White-line fever, running the lines, the half-back line, the boundary line, the party line, lines in the sand, interchange lines, even the opening line of your club song. Whatever your line, we cannot escape them.

If you remove the definitive white lines from a footy field, all we are left with is a big patch of grass. (Not to be confused with patchy grass, I might add.) Or are we? There are heaps of other lines, too. I reckon there are also lines that bind us: we can't see them quite as clearly as a boundary line, but they are just as real.

A few weeks ago, on a windswept Monday afternoon in Footscray, a small gathering of men wandered out onto the Whitten Oval to perform their weekly ritual of taking out a beaten-up Sherrin and having a kick.

These blokes are not a team, as such – not in any official capacity, anyway. No uniforms or signatures on insurance forms are required if you want to join them. They are just a motley group of footy lovers who enjoy nothing more than having a kick. Their preferred dungheap is Fitzroy's old ground on Brunswick Street, but on special occasions they make for various old suburban stages in search of an added touch of nostalgia or adventure.

The format is pretty simple; many of you will know it as circle work. Scattered out around the ground, the boys lead, mark, kick or flick it off by hands to keep the ball moving. It's all about keeping the flow of play alive.

No goals are scored. In fact, the whole thing moves along without any attention paid to the lines on the field. To say they do just fine without these markings is to do them an injustice. What they create every Monday afternoon is harmony. A football symphony, if you will.

Someday, I can see myself joining a football choir just like this one, a place where the rules and boundaries dissolve and the only focus is getting a touch and moving it on to the bloke upaways from me. But for now I'm pretty content in the hustle and bustle of the AFL.

Last weekend we had a pretty big game, big for many and varied reasons. As much as I love the whimsical romance of circle work with a group of football gypsies, there really is nothing to compare to being a part of a team, standing arm-in-arm in your colours and singing an ancient song at the top of your voice.

Footy is an emotional game, and it's the emotion it draws out of people that is its greatest strength. The pressure of last week was palpable, and on Sunday afternoon, deep down below Docklands, you could sense within the four walls that we had all leant on each other for support at some point during the previous days. That's not just player to player, but everyone at the Bulldogs. The machinery of a football club means that every soldier in every department pulls their little bit of weight to help the greater good and force the forward motion to continue.

In the first quarter against Fremantle, the 22 players who took the field were indeed the lucky ones. We got to show the end result of a club clawing its way inch by inch in the right direction. To the last minute of the game we played for our club and our jumper, and it was our reward to stand arm in arm and sing the club song. I can't remember a game where we all stood together and belted it out, and it was an enormous privilege to be part of.

Just looking around the circle made the hairs on my neck stand up. Why? Because we were experiencing a rare sense of togetherness that, unfortunately, you don't get in life all that often. It was hard not be moved by our property steward and club legend, Eddie Walsh, being helped into the circle, walking stick in hand, to play his richly deserved part in this show of unity.

But for me it wasn't just Eddie who filled me with a sense of pride. I was scanning the group and caught the eye of one of our newest staff members, osteopath Nick Brasher. He'd been dragged in as well, and the look on his face was one of shock, but also pride – he's one of us for life now. It didn't even matter that he was a bit sketchy on the words. All in good time.

People all week have asked about the significance of an entire club standing arm in arm, and I've sometimes had the feeling the answer they have been expecting is built around ideas of war or hatred. That's not the way I see it. The show of unity, standing together as one, was the show of a club at peace. The wars are fought out on the field, the song sung by free men and women.

Whether you're playing the game for four points or just to fill in a Monday afternoon, you should do it to be a part of something. If only for a moment.

29 July 2010

Circle work with a bunch of football gypsies
has become a staple of my off-season fitness campaign.
I look forward to it every year.

ADVICE THAT'S OUT OF THE (COACH'S) BOX . . . COUGH

All rugged up and assigned to statistics duties (having been ruled out with the Footscray flu), I was following Rocket and the assistant coaches through the Adelaide outer towards the coach's box. Then came a sweetly timed gem of advice from a new South Australian friend which made me laugh (a chuckle that soon escalated into another coughing fit): 'F—en eat something, Murphy!'

Ah, Adelaide, how I've missed you.

I guess this is the time of year to get sick, and not all of it ends in a coughing fit. While we've had some genuine ailments to worry about at the Kennel this week, there are plenty of people who seem a bit sick and tired of the whole seemingly choreographed election show.

After a patchy start, it looks as though Our Julia has taken charge of her own destiny; to use her own well-worn phrase, things are 'moving forward'. Sounds a bit like her favourite team at the minute. Cough.

Political leaning is a strange beast – asking someone who they follow in footy is fine, but it's too personal to ask which team they barrack for in Canberra. I come from Labor stock, and was brainwashed at the kitchen table at a young age.

But I'm an adult now, and I've got my own kitchen table to sit around and my own little ones to brainwash. So I took a moment this week to cut through all the backwash and see where my political heart lies.

To borrow a line from Nick Hornby's *High Fidelity*, if I may, 'it's not what you *are* like, but *what* you like' that is important. Then it hit me: Julia's favourite song is Springsteen's 'Born to Run'. There's my vote, end of story. It should've been her campaign slogan, now that I think of it. Get rid of 'Moving Forward' and roll out 'Born to Run'; could even get the Boss to sing a few bars!

How did I get here? The combination of Panadol and Lemsip seems to have left me a little disoriented, bouncing from Adelaide to the flu to the campaign trail. Back on subject.

All week I've been bunkered down, cut off from my Bulldog brothers in a quarantine not dissimilar to the movie *Outbreak* (although no monkeys are connected to this Footscray flu, I'm happy to report – at least, not at this stage). So, having been sent to the equivalent of footy's sick bay last Sunday, I got to watch my boys slip, slide and skid to an important interstate win.

Sitting up in the coach's box watching your own team play is a pretty weird experience. The main thing you feel will come as absolutely no surprise: you want your boys to win. Simple. But something I noticed as a spectator is the admiration I have for the players. It's a tough, tough game, and sitting out for a week takes you to a different place altogether.

Out there, you have too many jobs to do, too many worries and considerations on your mind to be wondering out loud about your sport and your teammates. Watching Sunday's very tense last quarter filled me with enormous pride.

I keep going back to the image of the ball skidding towards the Adelaide goal-face, with only Kurt Tippett and Easton Wood to influence its fate. Easton kept his feet, danced around Tippett and took the ball away from danger. It was a huge moment in the game, and perhaps an even bigger moment in a career.

I also vow never again to sit with Leon Cameron at a Bulldogs game. He sees the game unfold like he is looking into a crystal ball, and tells you what's happened long before it occurs. When the scores are that close, it's like listening to Alfred Hitchcock predict the scary bits in *The Birds*.

So where does that leave us now? I plan on making my escape from quarantine any minute – I've had too much time away from the Bulldog brotherhood already for my liking. The People's Beard might be clean-shaven if I don't get back soon.

Sickness? Well, it passes, and we have much to do before September, starting with the Cats on Saturday night. Can't let the sniffles get in the way.

The mantra this week comes once again from our favourite Yank, Mr Springsteen, who told us we could hide 'neath the covers and study our pain, or take the alternative path. 'Show a little faith, there's magic in the night . . .'

12 August 2010

ANOTHER LONG WAIT
FOR A CUP BEGINS

So close yet so far. With eyes firmly fixed on the cup, in a flash it becomes apparent there is a long, dry summer ahead before we can have another tilt at it.

Slumped in the corner of a tiny room beneath the stands of the MCG, I put my head in my hands to will myself closer to the holy grail. But time has a knack of taking its, um, time – a post-match drug test can be as heartbreaking as the game, especially if you can't produce enough for a sample.

In the hours before my stalled drug test, my Bulldogs and I once again fell short in the week before the big one. Deja vu in many ways, but no less painful the third time around.

The protocol for a drugs test stipulates that you must produce 90 millilitres of your finest in a small beaker – which, under normal circumstances, would be no trouble at all. But after a game of football (a Prelim, no less), 90 millilitres can feel like 90 litres.

I took my beaker into the bathroom, with my anti-doping

authority minder for company, and stepped up to the plate. Moments later we were both looking dejectedly at the evidence, our spirits fading in the same way Footscray hopes had faded an hour earlier. Twenty millilitres, maybe 25. My hopes of providing an adequate sample were starting to look a bit like trying to win the Premiership from eighth position – not impossible, but you need things to go your way.

For 25 weeks things have fallen into place for the Magpies and Saints. Having played both teams in the past few weeks, I'm in a reasonable position to predict that we'll see a classic Grand Final on Saturday.

Like all good teams, the Saints and Pies work like big, heavy machinery – once they kick into gear, they are very hard to stop or shift off their path. The Magpies, especially, have a knack of hitting their stride from the opening moment of the match. Can they burst out of the blocks on the biggest stage? It's not as easy to do that for three games in a row as some would have you believe.

I will say this, though: if early on we see the Carringbush go from deep in defence and carry the ball all the way, with names like Heath Shaw, Scott Pendlebury, Dane Swan, Alan Didak and Travis Cloke all getting a touch and moving it on quickly, the alarm bells should sound for Saints supporters.

The Saints, an impressive machine themselves, took a bit longer than the Pies to find their rhythm against us on Saturday night, but were no less formidable when they did. I don't think the Saints will have the luxury of fumbling chances in front of goal this year. Stephen Milne and the underrated Adam Schneider seem hell-bent on giving St Nick the support he deserves in the forward end.

If Collingwood is like a bulldozer, destroying everything in its path, then perhaps St Kilda is more of a Central Park Christmas tree, each branch fitting in snuggly with the next. But to make the tree a thing to behold, a star must sit atop, shining brightly for all to see. Nick Riewoldt is that star, and any side with the big number 12 would be a chance, bulldozer or not. And so it comes down to two: a bulldozer and a tree. Who'd have thought football could get even more political?

It's between two but about one, that being the cup itself. Like this lonesome columnist sat in the bowels of the MCG willing his bladder to the magical 90-millilitre mark, these two teams will be wanting to fill the cup, albeit with something more palatable – champagne and the spoils of victory.

It will taste as sweet as ever, I imagine. For the Bulldogs and plenty more, that's all we can do – imagine.

As the clock ticked on to quarter to midnight on Saturday, when all had left the MCG, I was still sat there with my minder and a virtually empty beaker. After seven bottles of water and some jogging on the spot, still nothing. We hatched a plan to put my hands under running water to speed up the process. Amazingly, it worked. It was a team effort by this stage, and we sailed past the 90-millimetre mark until the beaker almost overflowed.

What does that tell us about footy? Probably nothing, but for the rest of us who aren't playing this Saturday, it might just mean that we have to wait a little bit longer and try some new things if we want to fill the cup.

23 September 2010

2011

DECIDING ON THE RIGHT TIME TO PUT IN THE BOOT

In the words of Larry David, that was brutal. Who'd have thought the first round of the AFL rollercoaster would be such a steep knee-trembler for the Dogs? Still, we have time on our side, but do we have timing? We'll come back to that.

It must be footy season again, because the restless nights are back and my feet look like they've been to 'Nam. I find it hard to let go of footy boots; I guess it would be fair to say I get emotionally attached to them.

After dusting myself off from the Bombers' raid last Sunday, I took myself down to the local sports store to buy some new boots – or 'wheels', as the young kids like to call them. I remember the days when boots would arrive in my locker at the club like they'd been left by some kind of grown-up Santa Claus. I buy my boots these days, while new 'wheels' get delivered almost daily to the pups out at the Kennel.

It took a while, but I finally found a pair of black footy boots. I felt pretty chuffed as I carefully placed them on the counter.

'Are you a footballer?'

This can be a tricky one to answer, especially after a pummelling like the one we took on Sunday.

'Ah, yes, on my better days I am,' I replied nervously.

'You boys get a 30 per cent discount here,' the assistant said.

'Oh, really?' I feigned surprise. 'That's handy.'

We fake-laughed in unison.

'Can you sign this footy for me?'

'No problem.'

To think that only ten minutes earlier I'd been dreading this little chore of boot shopping. There was a pause from my clerk friend before he lifted his head and looked me in the eye. 'Didn't play well yesterday . . .'

Oh dear. Silence hung in the air like fog. I've been through this process a few times, and I know where it's headed. My palms began to sweat. 'Yeah, nah, it, um, wasn't too good, was it?'

'Pin or sign?'

A sigh of relief; we were back in business. 'I always sign – it's more retro.'

No laugh from my sales assistant friend. This was disconcerting; I usually get a laugh. 'Who'd you play on?'

Sweat dripping now. 'Oh, a few different blokes – they played well, didn't they? Always next week, blah, blah, blah . . .'

The Bombers gave us a lesson, but this clerk had crystalised it for me – when it comes to football and footwear, success is reliant on paying the price. The full price.

'Transaction approved.' I moved swiftly away, almost forgetting my boots. Timing is everything.

I've been thinking about timing all week. Timing in football used to mean the right time to push off a man and lead into space, while your teammate spotted you and kicked the ball out in front. An old coach of mine used to call this 'kicking the ball into an open window of a moving train'.

'Timing' is back in vogue lately – not the deft touch of when to nudge an opponent with your hip, but the right moment to unleash your substitute into the game. (Is it just me, or does anyone else have trouble saying 'substitute' without breaking into The Who's version?)

Back on topic: timing. On my travels this week I was back in my old home town for a club appearance – at the local supermarket, of all places. I had a few minutes to kill so I took my little mate Jarvis down to Civic Park to chase the birds and reminisce a bit.

When I was in primary school, around the age of ten or 11, I used to hang out at the park with a couple of mates. The thing was, these two mates had girlfriends and I didn't, so on the odd occasion that the girls would join us, it was my job to time them (with a stopwatch) kissing. On recall, it sounds a bit creepy and I do feel some trepidation about writing it, but it was all very innocent and quite wonderful in its own way.

The longer the kiss, the better – romance was not high on the agenda, as far as I could tell. The substitute rule is pretty low on romance, too, but it's got us players gasping for air.

So what about the Dogs? Round One is gone, and with it the chance of an early four points. We lost by plenty of points, but those ones won't matter – yet.

After a bad loss, the timing of Round Two couldn't be better. Onwards and upwards. Kiss kiss.

31 March 2011

WE DON'T HAVE THE RIGHT TO SHACKLE KRAKOUER

Mistakes are inevitable in life, and even more so in sport. Having played a bit of cricket growing up, I saw plenty of mistakes some with the ball – some with the bat, and a plethora in the field.

On one particularly hot afternoon on the country dung-heap in Hallora, just outside Warragul, a catch was put down by a teammate of mine to a collective groan. I'm not sure if there is a worse feeling in sport than dropping an easy catch on the cricket field. After the catch went down, and the echo of our unsympathetic despair had drifted off into the paddocks, our most senior cricketer spoke up: 'The only bloke who never made a mistake didn't play this game.'

I was 16 and filling in for the senior grades, and this bloke with the supportive words was in his mid-50s. I spent the rest of my afternoon in the outfield thinking about what he'd said and what he meant. In a way, I've never really stopped thinking about it. So, who was this bloke who never made a mistake?

By the time the bails were flicked off that evening, the 16-year-old boy staring out across the paddocks had concluded that the wise old head on our team must have been referring to Jesus. He seemed to keep his nose pretty clean, and there was no mention of cricket at Mass on Sundays. Some 12 years later, I'm not so sure if there is someone out there with a soul so pure.

Mistakes are just a part of life for all of us, aren't they? We can all identify when people come up short, when souls are flawed, but few of us can know what it's like when the mistake you make becomes a matter for the law, and your penance a prison sentence.

Andrew Krakouer is a seriously good footballer. He was laconic at Richmond and showed glimpses of genius, but to survive in footy these days, teams require more than flashes of gold. They demand a steady stream of nuggets.

Like many, I've watched his comeback with interest, and have been amazed and indeed inspired by his play. Watching last Friday night, I also saw his gesture to the crowd, hitting his wrists together in a moment of celebration.

In the following days, I was surprised to find this gesture being picked apart, with questions even being raised as to whether the AFL should step in and ban it. I found the hypocrisy of the whole thing quite unsettling.

Here we have a man who has paid his debt to society and been roundly celebrated for overcoming some major hurdles to once again shine on the footy field. And how do we react when he dares to make reference to his time in prison?

For many, this was far too in-your-face and not to be tolerated: 'No, no, Andrew. We're happy for you to be back playing football, now that you're all nice and neat. But please, there's no need to drag us back into your grubby prison cell. Especially not live on TV – there are kids watching, you know.'

It seems many followers of the game are happy enough to see Krakouer back, but feel like they have a right to dictate the terms. If he keeps his nose clean and plays nice footy, that's okay. But they're appalled when he indulges in what may have been a moment of emotional release, his own little celebration of how far he has come. Or perhaps it was as simple as sending good wishes to his brother, who is in a Perth prison. I think he's justified on both counts.

Questions must be asked about the symbol itself. I don't know Krakouer at all, and his gesture could be taken a number of ways. But one thing I'm sure of is that it wasn't a gesture designed to celebrate his crime. If that was the case I could understand the outcry on the street, but I'm certain that's not what he had in mind.

AFL players have all sorts of pressures in their lives, not just as footballers but as human beings. Relationships, injuries, poor form, kids who won't go to sleep, illness, etc. It's our job as professionals to overcome them and play to an acceptable standard. It's when we manage to do this really well that you see some sparks of emotion flying on the field. Fist-pumping, hugging, smiles, shouts of joy.

Krakouer spent 16 months in prison, and some of us won't afford him the luxury of what I saw as a sign of freedom. His is an uncommon comeback story. All the more reason that the man and his freedom ought to be celebrated out loud, like the cries of someone who's just struck gold.

14 April 2011

MODERN ADVENTURES CAPTURE CITY'S SPIRIT

'When I hear that whistle blowin', I hang my head and cry . . .'

Oh, how I miss catching the train. What else connects you to your city more than to be a commuter of a morning?

I loved those frosty mornings, walking to the station with my Thermos in hand, newspaper at the ready and Johnny Cash and his ilk providing the soundtrack for the journey. It was an adventure, a modern version of Huck Finn's raft, I thought.

I felt more a part of the city then than ever. Of course, with that I also became part of the commuter team, joining the collective groans and curses when the announcement of another train delay would inevitably snap the romance like a twig. But I was connected, and that's important.

The trouble with having gypsy blood is you tend to move around a lot. After spending a year out in the north-eastern suburbs, where I could indulge my love of the rail, my little gang is back in more familiar territory, amid the hippies, drunks and urban decay. It's good to be back; I just wish a train ran from Princes Park to Whitten Oval.

Being stuck in traffic along Flemington Road is not exactly the Mississippi, and I'm feeling less and less like ol' Huckleberry with every passing day.

With a rare weekend off for the bye, I thought I would get along to Friday night footy at the 'G to reconnect with my city. I'm still a little grey on what it means to be Australian, and I'm downright baffled as to what it means to be 'un-Australian'. But I do know what it means to be a Melburnian.

I took great delight in hopping on the tram and heading into the city to meet a friend. We walked to the ground with the other pilgrims: cocky little Magpies leading the way, and some rather nervous Tiger cubs visualising what might lie ahead for their team. It took me back.

Sitting up high in the Great Southern Stand was a thrill, and one I hope never dulls. Collingwood was impressive. From my lofty vantage point, the players' faces were a blur, robbed of the emotions that would normally greet me like a slap. But the way they marshalled themselves as a defensive unit was impressive, and they strangled the younger Tigers early, like a boa would a fledgling frog.

The Age's Martin Flanagan likes to sit near the fence so he can get a feel for the intensity of the contest, hearing and feeling how hard the bodies hit each other. And I agree with him that it's a much different game the closer you get. But it was educational for me to see the little black and white ants scurry the ball into the forward pocket and begin the stranglehold.

Those little frogs I mentioned, though, the Tigers, showed a bit of fight, and for 15 minutes in the third quarter they took on the big boa with bold kicking and playing on through half-back. They made the Magpies look a little uncomfortable.

As the Tigers flirted with the idea of getting up on the shoulder of the Magpies, the crowd lifted, and with each promising forward thrust they were heaving. Minutes later, Dale Thomas ran the length of the ground and the contest died again. That, too, brought back memories for an ex-Tiger devotee.

The next day was indie record store Saturday, and I was down at the local park with the little ones. All day I was gushing about the tangerine beauty of an autumn afternoon in Melbourne. Just gorgeous. After my third outburst of, 'Look at the colours of the sunshine on those trees, honey!' Jarvis's mum said, 'That's enough!'

My autumn glow was soured somewhat when word filtered through that my music shop of choice, the Last Record Store, was looking down the barrel of ultimate defeat. If there is indeed such a thing as 'un-Australian', then letting these sacred places go under is surely it.

Connecting with your record store is connecting with your city, and whether you're riding the rails or cheering from the stands, it's the connection that's important. Do your bit. Make your next train trip to your local record store.

21 April 2011

BADS, BIG BADS AND SHOCKERS: WELCOME TO ZONEBALL

'Zoneball is a game invented by bored musicians, and is basically a cross between tennis and footy. It was codified by Tex Perkins on October 14, 2001. Popular with cripples, musos and comedians, it can be played whilst drunk (the one-handed aspect of the game allows players to drink, smoke or eat as they play). It is truly the game of the 21st century.' So said Tex Perkins in May 2011.

While Tex is to zoneball what Tom Wills is to footy, I only became aware of the game about 12 months ago. I have since joined the small but loyal group of disciples more than willing to spread the gospel of its appeal to the masses.

A few years back I innocently filled out a player profile form for the *Footy Record* and was asked who my dream dinner guests would be. I put down my newest friend at the time, Gus Agars (a drummer of some repute), along with a couple of other gunslingers, Tim Rogers (whom I'd met a couple of times) and Tex Perkins (whom I'd never met).

I didn't think much more of it until it finally appeared in the *Footy Record* and someone passed it on to Gus, who got a laugh out of it. End of story, or so I thought.

A few weeks later I was summoned to a midweek dinner at Tiamo in Lygon Street. Waiting at the table were – as you have probably guessed – Tim, Tex and Gus. I was both tickled and pink. How many people can say they have actually broken bread with their dream dinner guests?

We chatted, ate and drank, and for the most part I didn't feel like a starstruck super-fan, which was a nice surprise. Two things I remember from that night: firstly, Tim ordered chicken livers, which fascinated me; secondly, a large portion of the table conversation centred on this phenomenon called zone-ball. By the end of the night I had been given a full rundown not just of the rules but also of the ethics that make up zone-ball, its history and its future. Just like with the chicken livers, I was intrigued.

Many weeks passed before rumours of a reunion surfaced. We were to meet at Edinburgh Gardens for an exhibition of zoneball, and a quick refresher course was needed.

The ethics: opposing players must bow to each other before the start and at the completion of every match, demonstrating the ceremony of battle and the respect between warriors.

The rules: two opponents face off, and you serve by kicking the ball and trying to land it in your opponent's court. Your opponent attempts to catch the ball, but only with one hand. If your serve lands outside the court, this is a 'bad'. Two bads in a row is a point conceded. A marked bad is two points. A 'shocker' is when a serve fails to leave the server's zone, and is worth two points. A 'big, bad shocker' is when your opponent marks the ball in your zone. (This is rare and worth three points.)

What's intriguing about zoneball is that the way you play the game often mirrors how you are in life. Take my dream-team dinner party crew, for example:

Gus Agars: Generally quiet on the court, but a fierce competitive streak bubbles just below the surface. A good player, too, maybe even the best there is. Has a penchant for headbands that lends him a Bruce Doull-ishness. Has style and substance.

Tex Perkins: The creator, the maestro, the master of ceremonies. Watch Tex in the throes of zoneball and you find yourself thinking, 'theatrical' and 'dramatic'.

Very early in my education, I leaned across to Tim and said, 'Each time Tex goes near the ball it's like an event in itself – a lot of grunting and involuntary movement of the limbs.'

Tim whispered in reply, 'Tex is like that away from zoneball. Cooking, for instance, same thing.'

Not just the creator and a good player, Tex is also the most renowned umpire of zoneball. I still recall him screaming at me, 'Did it touch your testicles?' It had, and I lost the point. Only your hand may touch the ball.

Tim Rogers: A gifted player with R&B – not rhythm and blues, but rhythm and bounce, which for a staunch Kangaroos man has a certain irony. Is more enamoured with acknowledging the gifts of other players than his own, but when he loses himself 'in the zone' it's a beautiful thing to behold.

As for me, I'm just a baby in terms of zoneball, but I'm working on the basics and my bow is coming along. I hope to change the way zoneball is played with the introduction of my 'floater' serve; it's a work in progress.

The four of us now meet semi-regularly for a feed, and it's always thrown together at the last minute; it's a bit mad but always a laugh. I thought chicken livers was an unusual thing to order, but at our most recent gathering Tim asked for seven oysters. I eagerly await his next request.

But what about the here and the now? The Bulldogs have had a couple of bads, as Tex would say, but all is not lost. One thing that rock 'n' roll, footy and zoneball have in common is that anything can happen.

We face Geelong on their home soil this week, and we will bow to them and they to us. And so another battle will begin.

2 June 2011

I am still perfecting the floater. When I do,
it will *change the way zoneball is played forever.*

I'LL FIGHT TO HELP DOGS ESCAPE A DARK PLACE

One of my favourite films is *Thirteen Days*, which covers the inner workings of a JFK-led government through the Cuban missile crisis in 1962. With the world on the brink of a nuclear catastrophe, and being misled from within by his own military officials, who want a war at any cost, JFK makes a confession to his brother Bobby: 'I woke up today and had forgotten about all this, and for a second I wished someone else was president . . .'

Bobby realises the gravity of these words: 'Do you mean that?' he says softly, as if fearing his brother's response so much he can barely say the words.

JFK looks his closest confidant in the eye and replies: 'I said "for a second".'

Just for a second this week I wondered about being an AFL player. Just for a second.

I have this place – it's a beautiful place and very real. If I was to give you a map or directions you could certainly go there if you had the time and inclination, but it's also a place of my imagination. I've been to this place many times. The first was on a holiday with Jarvis and Frankie's mum, and we took off in the car for a bit of a wander. Like all good things in life, we stumbled upon it almost by accident.

This place was just so full of life. The smell of fresh sea air, the smooth, rounded, green hills that went on and on, and the warm sun on our faces. Something shifted for us that day. It felt like home, and also like something totally new, a beautiful juxtaposition.

This place is a 15-minute drive inland from the coast, along a road that weaves up through the rolling hills. I like driving, and when the scenery is so calming I'd be happy to drive this road for days. Each year we try to get back there for a short stay to recharge the batteries, to get a clearer look at our lives. Every so often I find myself up in those hills, only this time in my imagination, and each time I visit, I add something new.

At first it was a little weatherboard shack on the side of a hill. The next time I threw in a view of the fuzzy coastline from the porch. Soon there was a chimney with plumes of smoke ascending into the evening sky. Most recently I've added a vegie patch to sit alongside the chicken coop.

I see this place with crystal clarity. I really don't know if it will be ours one day; it might just be a metaphor. But when I close my eyes this feels like the place for me and my family, once this hurly-burly life of AFL football has been exhausted.

For our team and supporters, this season has been a shock to all of us. I've grown to expect the unexpected in this caper, but who could have predicted the place we find ourselves in now? League footy is a high-pressure, cut-throat game. It's not a missile crisis, but it doesn't feel that far off when you're inside it.

Just like the Kennedy administration, we're all under the microscope and under attack from a broad range of enemies, some even posing as friends. We need people of action, people of will and people with the ability to keep calm under fire. Soldiers who will turn the tide, players who will keep trying until their last breath.

Today is my 29th birthday, but it's hardly a time to break out the party-poppers. Yet I will not give up hoping, and I won't stop trying. Because that is what we do: we strive to be better, and ultimately to win. It doesn't always go our way, but ain't that life?

I have this place . . .

Returning home up the highway after a belting at the hands of Geelong, I couldn't help but drift off to that magical place. For the briefest of moments I even put myself and my inner sanctum there, and it was just as I'd expected – perfect.

The flashing headlights zooming the other way brought me back to the present, and the reality that the Dogs are in football hell right now. I confess my guilt to my comrades at having left them, even for such a brief moment. And I vow to not let my focus stray again, not until this thing is completely exhausted. All I can ask at this time is that everyone in red, white and blue does the same.

That place in the hills can wait.

9 June 2011

FOOTY'S A PLACE
FOR TRUE COLOURS

Night games are tough on the kids. Take them along and they're exhausted for days, leave them at home and you risk breaking their little hearts.

Jarvis doesn't quite get football yet. Don't get me wrong, he loves his Bulldogs, but it's all the other details that seem a bit fuzzy to him. For instance, he thinks I go off to work at Woofa's house every day. He's not wrong, it's just fuzzy.

Last Friday evening, as I was packing my bag in preparation for battle against the Demons, Jarvis sidled up to me, entwined an arm around my leg and asked, 'I go with Dad to football?'

It was hard to find the right words. 'Not tonight, mate. You stay with Mum and Frankie. We'll go to the footy tomorrow.'

I'm not sure who was more confused: Jarvis (in his Bulldogs jumper, no less), wondering why Dad wouldn't take him to Woofa's house, or me, who up until a few moments ago had a footy-free weekend.

I woke up the next morning (after our magnificent win

against the Dees) to the sound of tiny feet shuffling up the hallway. And then this little face peered over my doona with the excited expression you usually find on children at Christmas time. 'We go to the football today, Dad?' It was 6.12 am.

After the strongest of coffees, I asked around and fortunately a few Bulldogs people were heading along to the MCG to watch the Tigers take on the Blues. Our day was set – we were off to the footy.

Bulldogs assistant coach Brett Montgomery met us and we all hopped on the train. At this point it's worth noting that, after some strong discouragement from his dad, young Jarvis was still dressed head-to-toe in his favourite Bulldogs get-up.

Jarvis's mum and I had a little side bet on what point in the day our little Bulldog would realise he wasn't actually going to watch the Bulldogs. I was pretty sure from the looks we were getting from the football commuters that the penny would drop before our packed train reached its destination. Nothing from the little man, though – there were snacks to be devoured.

The game itself was a bit of a fizzer, and by half time things were already looking ominous. The Tigers didn't seem as mighty as they have been at various stages this year, and the Blues shone so bright they hurt my retinas. They know what they're doing out there, and they also have Chris Judd. That never hurts.

As the little leaguers ran around doing their thing, I felt compelled to ask my son who he was barracking for – the Blues or the Tigers? He gave me a confused look and replied: 'Dogs.' I was losing that bet with his mum.

By three-quarter time the lead had blown out, the snacks were all gone and we decided to beat the masses and catch the early train home. We weren't alone in our thinking, as a sea of bodies splashed in yellow and black poured out of the MCG like overflowing water from a reservoir.

The gate attendants were almost drowned out by the crowd noise, but I heard one of them say, 'If you want to come back in, you'll need a pass out!' Some Tiger fans standing nearby thought that was pretty amusing. They'd seen enough.

We pushed our way onto the crowded train and took a moment to reflect on the day. The game wasn't a classic, but it was still a day at the footy with my little mate, and that'll always be a good day. The constant sideways rocking of the train carriage sent me drifting away, and I got to thinking about the upcoming week and my old mate Lindsay Gilbee playing his 200th game against the Blues. It will be a huge game for us, and for Gilbs.

I remember hearing Dermott Brereton once say that anyone who has played 200 games of league footy has a daily reminder when he's finished. I think he was referring to the bumps and bruises accumulated over ten-plus years at the elite level.

There are other forms of great loss that leave no physical scars, but are no less painful. Gilbs knows this better than most. All of his Bulldog brothers are very proud of him.

As Jarvis and I walked hand in hand off the train and down the platform, I got to thinking how football is many things, but often it's just a place to be with your nearest and dearest. Other times it's a place to remember those you love who have passed on to somewhere else. It's also a place to wear your true colours, no matter who's playing. My boy taught me that.

7 July 2011

HEAVY QUESTIONS WITH FEW ANSWERS

In the aftermath of our defeat at the hands of Essendon last Saturday night, I was asked to speak to the ABC Radio team. As soon as I put the 'cans' on, I had the feeling the ABC guys were in the throes of dissecting the flaws of my team. I'd walked into a mini-storm.

I stood in the empty changerooms feeling like an opening batsman facing the first over of a Test match – ducking, weaving, defending, leaving some for the keeper, until finally you get a ball that is almost unplayable.

The respected former coach and football identity David Parkin prefaced his question by saying it might be too tough to answer straight after a game, but then went on to ask: 'Where is the team at?' (He might have said 'club' instead of 'team', I can't remember.)

Parkin was a revered coach, and he would have made an excellent fast bowler, too. It was a difficult question, and after trotting out some clichéd truths – good young players, untimely injuries, etc. – I admitted the possibility that, yes, perhaps we were in a transition of sorts, and that ultimately I had just as many questions as they did.

Yesterday marked yet another transition. The club's decision not to renew Rocket's contract has left everyone pretty well stunned – not least the man himself, I suspect.

Rocket's future has been a story all year. As a player, you are aware of the speculation, but it still knocks you on your backside when the axe falls.

After Allan Jeans passed away a few weeks ago, I wrote about the relationship between a coach and his players. Although Yabby and Rocket seem quite different in lots of ways, it is that overwhelming influence they have on their players that leaves us shocked when time is called.

I watch a lot of Friday night football. Often I watch the speed with which the ball and the players move and think to myself, 'I'm not sure I'm up to that,' even though I know I've been doing it for years. In many ways, a coach is the person who instils that belief in you to be more than what you think you're capable of being; someone who persuades a group of men and boys who endure bouts of self-doubt to pool together and realise what they could be as a team.

Those fears of 'not being up to it' affect most players, but a will to win the respect of their coach is always a driving force. Since 2005 Rocket has been that person for me and my Bulldog teammates.

All your actions on a football field influence those around you. Sometimes the best reward can be a nod or a wink from the coach, a pat on the back as you leave the field. When I was done with my media duties last Saturday, I went back into the locker room and the People's Beard asked me if I fancied a beer. It seemed like the thing to do to raise a glass to our fallen comrade Dale Morris, and to stop the questions swirling.

'So much older . . . than I was . . . yesterday.' It's a powerful thing to hear a song that captures the way you feel at a certain moment. As I drove home listening to Tex Perkins and the Dark Horses, it was hard not to feel like this season had slipped away. Parkin's question – 'Where is the team at?' – swished around my head.

I walked into our cosy local, and there were plenty of regulars enjoying their Saturday night. One, Rose, greeted me with a hearty, 'Great win tonight!' Her bloke, Flynn, was quick to whisper in her ear that, in fact, the Dogs had lost.

Even with the buzz of the pub, that question was still knocking back and forth between my ears. Thankfully, another one cut through the noise like a knife: 'Fancy a Cooper's?' Ah, finally a question with an easy answer!

By my third ale, the text came from the Beard that he wouldn't be able to make it, and that felt like my cue to excuse myself. After a Chevy Chase moment – 'I was so hungry I could eat a pie from a gas station' – I sat on my front doorstep and let the question rattle around further.

It's strange to imagine someone else in charge at the club. In 2005 many of us were just boys; now, those who remain are husbands, fathers, veterans. It is the end of an era, just shy of the golden era of success we all dreamt of. Next year I will turn 30 and play under my fourth coach at the Bulldogs. The need to replace questions with answers will be supreme.

Through the fog we find ourselves in now, there will be new challenges, a new voice, and perhaps, if everything falls into place, a golden era ahead. But for now we will play out the season with the man who convinced his boys for seven years that they were up to it.

18 August 2011

FAREWELL TO THE PEOPLE'S BEARD

Beards are flying at half-mast today as a tribute to our retired comrade, Ben 'the People's Beard' Hudson.

The decision has come as a shock to many of his admirers. It's fine for Ben to retire, but the beard that has long adorned his face is, in fact, the property of the people. For some, you sense there will never be closure. Still, it might be best to move on from the messy endings of such matters and just raise a glass or, indeed, a razor to one of our favourite Bulldogs and his trusty, hairy sidekick.

The pre-season in the summer of 2007–08 was a very tough time. We'd been smacked very badly in the last half of the '07 season. Throw in the fact that our new facility wasn't quite ready for use, and it was very much a case of back to basics. Everyone at the club had been put on notice, and those long summer training sessions were a grind of body and mind. Funnily enough, we had recruited well, and 'Huddo' headed up that list.

I'm not sure what he made of the conditions which he

encountered on his arrival at the Kennel, but moving from the Crows' pristine facilities to our campsite must have been an eye-opener. True to the man, he never once gave the impression that he was anything but excited to be on board. Recruiting older players is not an exact science. Some just don't work out, some go loopy and write books, while others, like Huddo, take it upon themselves to make it work. It took him about three days to find his feet; from then on it felt like he had been there for years.

He moved into a house around the corner from me, and pretty soon we were sharing rides to training. We had common ground, too: he let me play Johnny Cash, we both liked coffee, and we indulged in the extreme sport of driving our cars with the petrol gauge on empty, for the simple thrill of seeing if we could make it. We did eventually come unstuck, and came to a grinding halt under a railway bridge in West Footscray. We both cheered when the car chugged to its final resting point, which confused anyone who happened to be driving past, but we felt like we'd reached the summit of our sport. We never got that Premiership Cup we wanted so badly, but we'll always have that moment of glory.

What made the People's Beard such a great teammate and clubman was that he made footy fun, and that's not something you always associate with footy any more. When he wasn't pushing the petrol gauge, the Beard gained most of his enjoyment from his thirst for competition.

I've always thought that sledging was one of the most overrated parts of the game, but Huddo didn't just make it an art form, he used it as fuel.

You won't find a more relaxed footballer away from the

field than big Huddo, and that laid-back attitude would occasionally roll out onto the training track. 'Gia' would often wind him up by saying, 'You're a woeful trainer.' That would usually be enough to get a rise out of Huddo, and his competitive nature would bare its teeth.

But nobody needed to prod him when it came to the real stuff. The Beard needs competition and physical combat like the rest of us need oxygen. I pity his first opponent in mid-week basketball next year. Those five fouls will be gone in a wink.

The Beard is a self-deprecating kind of guy. When I asked him yesterday to describe himself in three words, he said, 'Graceful, efficient, delicate and classy.' Despite his intriguing take on numeracy, you can take from his sarcasm that the Beard was no delicate flower on the field. You won't see him in the contenders for mark or goal of the year, but to suggest he had limited skills is not showing enough appreciation for the man or the game. His great talent was to wrestle the ball our way and bring his 'classier' teammates into the game. His skill set borrowed more from heart and soul than glossy highlight reels.

I was once asked what made the Beard a footballer, and I replied, 'He makes his teammate a better player.' I was right, but I stopped short. He made his club better too.

As he runs out of petrol, we should all stop and cheer. It's been a great ride.

25 August 2011

Every word in this column is true, except for the bit where the
People's Beard retires. As it currently stands, Ben Hudson
has retired three times and played at four clubs. All with a beard.

SEASON'S END IS DESPERATE AND DARTLESS

Performing under intense pressure makes up a large of proportion of what league footy is all about, but what about when the season comes to an early, bitter end? Well, out west we usually turn to a game of darts to get our pressure-cooker fix.

I've grown to hate the phrase 'Mad Monday'. For mine, 'wake' is a much better description of the final nail in your season's coffin. A few years back, after another early finish, someone came up with the ingenious plan to put our team poster on the wall and throw darts at it. Each player would get one dart, and in number order you had to step up to the line ('toe the oche', I believe the darts aficionados say), and throw your missile at a face of your choosing.

The rules are simple: if your dart hits a player, he receives a penalty in the form of a beverage. If you hit the coach, you may pick a player you think is in need of refreshment. Hit yourself and you've earned a double whack. If your dart misses the poster completely . . . well, you don't want to know what's in store.

The pressure is really on, too. Nervously you stand, dart in hand, and line it up with your good eye closed. Behind you, a chorus of abuse builds as teammates will your projectile to sail wide of their image and fall somewhere, anywhere else.

My all-time favourite darts moment features former team-mate Tim Callan. Timmy stepped up to the plate, and just as he was about to launch his dart, he leaned over to me and whispered in my ear. His words will stay with me forever: 'I haven't hit the poster in three years.'

His voice was calm, in contrast to the wall of sound behind him. As Timmy braced himself and finally let go, the noise evaporated. As we awaited the outcome, it was as if time stood still.

The noise that broke the silence was one none of us expected. As the dart stuck in the carpet on the floor, squeals of joy and disbelief filled the room. We'd never seen a dart miss the wall.

Behind Timmy and me, there were scenes of jubilation that wouldn't have been out of place at Rio's Carnival. We were laughing so hard I thought our appendixes were a chance to burst. Timmy's place in Bulldogs' darts history was secured.

That was last year. This year there would be no darts – we were all ready to go, but there was not a single dart in the pub. So the poster hung on the wall without a single puncture wound.

It summed up our year, in a way – not much has gone right. All football followers are excited by this time of year. The sun is out, and the best players in the best teams are running on top of the ground, as they say. There is little thought for the teams that have run aground. Melbourne will come alive this weekend, and there's not a player outside the eight who wouldn't hand in his hangover for a taste.

At the Bulldogs, the last few days have felt like the end of something, or perhaps it's the beginning of something. It's been a chance to sit and talk and try to make sense of what has been a pretty terrible year. Any day is a good day to have a beer with Huddo and Hally, but it was more poignant knowing this was their last dance. Both went out in style; their last games were pretty good too.

When we weren't searching for a dart to throw at our poster, or were lost in the land of in-jokes, there were moments of reflection. Cal Ward has always felt like a little brother, and his departure has hit us hard. At times over the last few days I think we all put our arm around him in part to protect him from the scrutiny, and maybe in a last, vain hope that we could keep him from going. Other times we just poked fun at his expense. And that was that. The two big boys have sailed into the sunset, and our little brother has moved out.

What are you going to do about it? It is what it is. There isn't enough time in footy to sit around feeling sorry for yourself – there's too much that needs to be done.

8 September 2011

2012

CHEERS TO A NEW YEAR, LOST AND FOUND

It only takes two little words to ruin a bushwalk: 'We're lost.'

My better half is a lot cooler in a crisis than I am, and even though her bare-bones reply – 'We're not lost; I know where we are' – lacked a specific solution, she didn't lack conviction, which is important in that situation, for morale anyway. It was that conviction that convinced me to call off the rescue chopper, and 30 minutes later we were safely back in our car. I conceded that, yes, I can be a little dramatic.

Football is a funny ol' thing, and I don't think I'll ever be able to fully understand it. Perhaps it's not meant to be understood. What I do find interesting is how the game in all its many guises seeps into your bones – and once it's in, it stays.

Last weekend was the last chance anyone inside the four walls of an AFL club will get some time away with families and loved ones to relax. I decided to take my girl away for a couple of nights to a cottage in the mountains; we prefer peace and quiet these days.

The thing that illuminates my imagination is that no matter how far away you go, or the things you may do to rest the body and spare the mind for a day or two, the game remains. I sat there on the weekend looking into an open fire with my novel on the go, but not a minute would go by where something wouldn't shimmer in my mind, behind the eyes. An image, a split-second of play, sometimes a flash of light or the sound of bodies hitting each other.

These moments are gone before you know what's what, but they can leave you with a fleeting sense of panic or elation. Other times you'll think more consciously about the game, your place in it, your club's place in it, or the great many shades that make up 'the game'.

Like many of you, I suspect, I've taken some time to just sit and think about Jim Stynes these past few days. That's the other thing about a life with football – sometimes we pray. I finished the last football year high up in the rolling hills of the Otways. That particular trip was a spiritual one – in a football sense, anyway – and I guess on reflection it would be fair to assume I felt a little lost.

It had been one of those years – 2011 was not a happy one for any Bulldog, so I'm guessing I wasn't the only one to head for the hills, or the bar, or wherever one seeks solace. Coach gets sacked, young star ups and leaves for Breakfast Point, some dear friends retire . . . all that can leave a young man pondering the bigger questions in a football life that leans on those important relationships. And there's always the small matter of winning and losing.

Six months later, with 2011 long since faded and the shiny new season about to begin, I was up in the hills again, this time Olinda. Aside from my brief and ill-advised bushwalk panic, I don't feel quite so lost now.

That's not to say I feel 'found' either, it's just that a sense of purpose has once again spread through my club. A new coach with a big presence, some eager young faces willing to step up, and let's not forget about a few oldies who are desperate to hang around a little while longer.

It's probably the same for most clubs at this time of year, except I don't care as much about most clubs – I care about mine. I suspect y'all feel the same way. Sláinte.

29 March 2012

POWERFUL MOMENTS GRIP A FOOTBALLER'S WORLD

The umpire holds that little red ball aloft and 30-odd thousand people circling the field of play lift as one, like a wave on a beach. A game of football rumbles to life.

From where I take my mark, next to my opponent, Aaron Davey, the ball looks small. In the drizzle and fading light it seems further away than it surely is. Thirty-six players fix their focus on that little red ball, feel the presence of opponents and teammates around them, and maybe the crowd too. In this moment, that football and the game itself become the most important things in your life.

Hours earlier, my car approached the MCG and life slowed to a crawl. It's a powerful moment in a footballer's world to look up at the Great Southern Stand, pause for a moment, then head underneath to the players' car park. It is the colosseum of modern times in this country, and you feel the weight of that privilege.

Like most players, I like to take a walk out on the ground before a game, but I must say it's extra special to be strolling across the MCG on your own, bouncing a ball, your mind swinging between a million thoughts and none at all, lost in a moment. I can't recall how long I spent walking around the empty field on this day, but I know at some point I stopped to try to make sense of a footballer's lot.

Having been at it a while now – over 12 years and with no premiership to show for it – I wondered if what I do has meaning to it, a deeper meaning. Three losses on the trot will play these kind of games inside an ageing athlete's mind. Best to leave those bigger questions for another day, so I just kicked the ball skyward out in front of me, and marvelled at how I still didn't know which way it would bounce. It's the torturer and the temptress in a nutshell.

I stopped to talk to three different Bulldogs people on my way back into the rooms, and each conversation centred on the one idea: 'How lucky are we to be here?' The MCG in the twilight has that effect on people.

We took to the ground for our warm-up and I couldn't help but be drawn in by the heartfelt tribute to Jimmy Stynes being played on the big screen. It gave extra weight to those pre-game conversations I'd had about gratitude at being present at this special place.

The game finally gets underway, and it's slippery, really slippery. Often at the MCG, if it rains for a short time then stops, the ball becomes sticky and players' skills can ascend to a symphony. But not today – the ball is like a cake of soap from go to whoa. On this night, the game's musical accompaniment becomes more punk rock than Vivaldi, but it endures to the last minute. Beauty has many faces.

Martin Flanagan says that football is theatre, and I agree with him. As the second half starts, a Shakespearean villain enters from right of stage in the form of Demon Lynden Dunn. I guess from the TV it probably looks like dodgem cars hitting into each other; the truth is not that far away from that, to be honest. I want to stop Davey, Lynden wants to stop me, and around and around we go.

At one point I interrupt the niggle to negotiate a deal: 'I'll let you keep hitting me for the next hour if you explain the moustache for me.' We squabble over the details of that contract for the remainder of the night.

My impact on the game drops away, but Davey (one freakishly good goal aside) is quiet also. Who wins? That one could go round and round too.

The game is a scrap in the best possible way, and the Dogs emerge with our first win of the year. On a wet night in the best stadium in the world, we shake hands with our combatants with what I hope is mutual respect, then we head under to sing our tribal hymn, arm in arm.

That's a footballer's lot when the going's good, and I reckon that has to mean something.

26 April 2012

BATTLING WITH INNER VOICES ON GAME DAY

I hear voices in my head. And when I say voices, I mean two of them – and that's roughly one too many. In an Olympic year we might be hearing a lot more about these kinds of voices. Whether you're a hurdler, a marathon runner or a footballer, part of the caper of any professional athlete is to wage war against the 'little man on your shoulder'.

I feel like it's the right time to introduce this little man. This column recounts his experience of last Friday, before, during and after the Dogs' game against Collingwood. As you'll soon see, he's quite the rascal . . .

Just look at him, a grown man in his lounge room rolling back and forth to stretch his ageing spine. I think he does it just to wind me up. He knows constant movement makes it hard for him to hear me. Why can't he just sit still so we can have a chat? It's not like I don't have empathy for the poor sod – I mean, he's been at it a long time now, 13 years or so, and that's bound to have taken it out of him. We are adversaries for the most part, but I have to dip the hat when I see him like this, deeply focused, in his own world, which he likes to call 'football purgatory'.

On game day, this bigger man under my feet sometimes likes to jot things down in a notepad. It's like he thinks that if he puts his thoughts on paper, it will keep me out of the conversation. Just now he's written something about purgatory. It's something to do with how he feels before a game, when he's in this hyper-focused state.

'Football purgatory: it's a bit like snorkelling in the shallows, you're neither submerged in a world of fish, coral and seaweed, nor are you in your more natural state of sun, wind and noise. You're stuck somewhere in the middle, observing the oddness of it all.'

Gee, this bloke waffles a load of old bollocks if you let him. Look out – he's on the move again. He pauses the TV as he gets up to leave. He's so predictable, ol' Lanky, as I like to call him. Always watches a movie he's seen a hundred times before a game (this week it's *For the Love of the Game*). A new movie, with all its potential twists and turns, would drain too much energy out of his (pea) brain, he reckons.

He bends down to put on his runners and headphones, but we've been doing this dance for so long he knows it's futile to even think the Black Keys can drown me out. As the music starts, we begin our waltz and I ask the first of many questions: 'Hey, Lanky, have you thought of all the things that could go wrong tonight?'

I have to give him credit, he's gotten better over the years at keeping me quiet. He's always on the move, ducking and weaving. We arrive at the ground and he's lost in a different world now – one of routine. A good routine will drown me out, and he knows it.

The game starts and the speed is blinding. You may not believe me, but when it's time to go to work, we work together. I'll ask him the odd question every now and then, like 'How much is it worth to you?' or 'How much are you willing to burn in the stomach for a win?' It's for his own good.

The game is tight, and as it nears the crescendo he has the ball in his hands. I start whispering, then talking, then yelling at him: 'Get the ball across to the other side of the ground! I don't care if you go back first or across, long or short, just get it there!'

A dilemma appears before him as Travis Cloke makes position in between the short option and the long one. His presence puts Lanky in enough doubt, and with his jelly legs the kick to the long option doesn't make the whole journey. Cloke marks it and slots the goal. The game plays out and the Pies run away with it. The noise of 38,000 people is loud, and I'm sure there are more than a couple baying for the blood of my Lanky, but I don't think he hears them.

He can hear me, though. And now, slumped on the floor of the changerooms, it's him who asks me a question: 'Wanna dance?'

10 May 2012

TRICK OF THE LIGHT, OR JUST ANOTHER STEVIE J TRICK?

'Grandpa, tell us again about the day you played on Stevie J . . .'

When people complain that there are no characters left in the game, I sometimes wonder if, for some, to be a character you have to play the fool. My answer to anyone holding up this argument is simple: Stevie J. Here is a character who is no fool. If he were a cocktail he'd be three parts genius and one part rascal.

A couple of Tuesdays ago, out at the Kennel, we were having a light kick-to-kick at the Barkly Street end when Coach McCartney walked past.

'Who've you got for me this week?' I asked.

There was barely a pause. 'Stevie J.'

I knew in an instant this was going to be no ordinary week. Stevie J doesn't do ordinary.

The strange thing is that over the past ten years or so, I don't recall us ever having been direct opponents. The assignment has usually gone to Dale Morris.

One of the things I love about playing on a half-back flank is that, by coming up against some of the most talented players in the game (Johnson, Cyril Rioli, Alan Didak, Mark LeCras, etc.), you get to see the game through their eyes – where they run and how far they will run to take hold of a game is as fascinating as it is hard to nullify.

One factor that makes Geelong such a popular champion team is that they just play – they have their style, which they've been perfecting for a long, long time, and they back themselves in to beat you. If the Cats were a racehorse they would be Might and Power – they will do what they've always done and lay it down from the start to see how far you're prepared to go to beat them.

I spoke to our backline in the lead-up to last Friday night's game and left them with a simple message: 'Come prepared to run.' It's easy to be distracted by the fringes of Geelong's forward half: the emergence of Hawkins, Stevie's tricks, their unselfish passing in front of goal, just to name a few. All of it is underpinned by their willingness to cover an enormous amount of ground.

The start of the game was manic. As a backman, it's easy enough to tell how we're defending up the ground: if it's going well, when the ball comes forward there's only one side of the ground for your opponents to work in; but if the pressure is a little off, then your opposition forwards have the full width of the oval in which to work you over.

Stevie J might like a beer, maybe even a punt on the races, but what he really loves is open space in the forward half so he can use his bag of tricks to lose you and find the ball. Early on Friday night, Stevie had acres to work in, which was a worry against someone who only needed a car space.

At one point, as I did what I could to stay close, he stopped, gathered, spun and handballed over his head. All that was missing was his cape. Although he was exerting an influence, I took some solace in the fact that he wasn't kicking any goals himself, and that more than a few of his touches were coming backward of centre.

When a free kick was paid against a Geelong player for holding the ball and Stevie took it upon himself to chat with the umpire over the concept of prior opportunity, I took up the argument with him. Before you knew it we were in deep discussion about the incident, and even looked up at the replay to help sort it out. We decided to leave further discussion until after the game. I'm not sure what the umpire made of our somewhat polite exchange.

Stevie was my responsibility when he came forward, but when he put himself in the centre square, as he often does, I would hand him over. By halfway through the third quarter he was the most influential player on the ground but still hadn't hurt us on the scoreboard. It was at this point that he turned to me and said, 'I've almost halfway run this flu out!'

It was a cheeky thing to say, a touch arrogant, and just a bit brilliant. The obvious seed he'd planted was: 'I wonder how he'd be going if he was feeling well?' And while all this was going on, a great game of footy was going back and forth, Dogs threatening and Cats pulling away.

In the last quarter Paul Chapman had a set shot from right on the arc, and to my horror I saw Stevie bob up out of nowhere in the forward pocket, hiding next to the point post. God only knows how he got there, but it was so sneaky that even Chapman didn't see him.

A minute later the chat started up again. 'Did you see me sneak on there through the interchange?' he asked.

'Clearly not,' was all I could say.

And then he smiled for the first time that night, and out the side of his mouth said, 'It was quite rascal-ish, wasn't it?'

How can you not love that?

Not long after, the Dogs came roaring home and threatened to steal the game. True to form, Geelong wasn't done with, and kicked clear once more.

With the game still in the balance but slipping out of our grasp, the ball flew out of a centre bounce with Stevie on the lead. It took everything I had to make a spoil, but the job wasn't finished. He gathered the loose ball, spun, cut and danced his way out of trouble, before firing off the obligatory no-look handball, my arms and legs flailing after him.

Then he sidled up to me one last time and said, 'I usually save that stuff for finals . . .'

I don't think he was saying all this to be arrogant or to rub it in. He just wanted to give me the whole show, the full Stevie J extravaganza.

He was best on ground but I felt like I could still hold my head up. And at least I'll have a pretty good story for my grandkids.

31 May 2012

At the end of the season, it emerged that the umpires had awarded Steve Johnson the three Brownlow Medal votes for his performance in this match, while yours truly took home the two.

A FATHER LOST
TO SONS
OF THE WEST

'Only truthful hands write true poems. I cannot see any basic difference between a handshake and a poem.'
PAUL CELAN

So the legend goes, once a man had shaken the hand of Frank Sinatra, he became a part of an esteemed group. As if he were part of an unspoken code among men. Out in Footscray, we've been blessed to have something similar. We've had Charlie Sutton, a man whose handshake was like a poem.

One of the first things you would do as a brand-new Footscray recruit was meet Charlie. I remember when it was my time, having just come off the training track, pale and nervous and still just 17. And there was Charlie, back at his beloved Whitten Oval in the middle of summer, with no one around really, introducing himself to players old and new.

I must've shaken Charlie Sutton's hand a few hundred times over the ensuing years, and every time it felt important. It felt special.

There are things as a Footscray footballer that are just there. EJ Whitten is still there – and I say this as a player who never met the man, but I feel his presence nonetheless.

Stand on the ground that bears his name and you can hear his passionate address to his tired players, slumped on the muddy field.

Chris Grant is an almost mythical figure, whose humility and gentle touch breezed through this place as a player and continues now as a board member. Tony Liberatore's grunt and undeniable spirit linger in our changerooms. Jack Collins is there when I open my locker. John Schultz, Doug Hawkins . . . the list goes on.

All of these great figures were celebrated again last Saturday week, at our Hall of Fame night. But it was Charlie's presence that night, brief and ailing, that stayed with you. Just as it always did, as much as he didn't want the moment to be about him.

With Charlie Sutton . . . as players, we felt him there. You felt the touch of his hand with the weight of history in its grip.

Footscray is unique in lots of ways. We're outsiders in a city dominated by football. Outsiders geographically, and outsiders in other ways too. Our only premiership came way back in 1954, and the struggle for that elusive second one is our story stripped to its bare bones. Our 1954 premiership players are our heroes, and Charlie was their hero.

I'm into the symbolism of things. I think about it a lot. I think about our club theme song all the time, and its opening line, 'Sons of the West', asks me a more profound question. If we are its sons and daughters, then who is our father? I don't think it's going too far to say that figure is Charlie.

Yesterday, a football club lost its father, and as sons of that club we are in mourning. Our story stripped bare is one of glory and of tragedy, but it's a story that continues. One premiership in over 100 years is a big cross to bear, but it also looms as the biggest carrot in the game.

When Charlie was inducted as the first Hall of Fame legend two years ago, he spoke as only he could about guts, determination and that thing beneath your shirt called heart: without it, you don't win. Sitting in a wheelchair, having come straight from his hospital bed, he said he had always been thrilled to do anything he could for the Footscray Football Club.

All of us in his family should put our weight behind trying to fulfil a promise, to do whatever it takes. It may take time, but we should never forget that we shook the hand of Charlie Sutton.

CHARLIE SUTTON

3 April 1924 – 5 June 2012

Played: 173 games from 1946–56, kicking 65 goals;
18 games for Victoria and captain-coached the Big V in 1952
Coached: 162 games from 1951–57 and 1967–68;
captain-coach of the club's only
VFL/AFL premiership team, in 1954
Won: 1950 Bulldogs best and fairest
Club president: 1978–81

6 June 2012

---

*A great honour was bestowed upon me when the
Sutton family requested that I read this column out at Charlie's
memorial service. A few days later, the Bulldogs played
Port Adelaide at home and won handsomely. Sometimes a win is
worth a lot more than just the four points.*

DOGS WITH TWO LEFT FEET LET DANCE PARTNERS DOWN

'She's not what I would call a pretty horse – she's a big girl.'
POMPOUS ENGLISH COMMENTATOR

I'm a deep sleeper, maybe even the deepest of all time. When I was six or seven and staying at my Aunty Mary's in Lockington, I fell off the top bunk and landed with an almighty thud but still didn't wake up.

One of the drawbacks of this slumber superpower is that on occasion I can emerge from the depths of my snooze and be utterly confused about where, when and who I am. Last Sunday was one of those mornings. I woke up in a heavy fog, and as I tried to work out my bearings, there was an unmistakable sense of dread in the back of my mind, and an image of a horse in the front of my mind.

Slowly, I began to put the pieces together. Like many of you, I had stayed up to watch our famous mare Black Caviar at Royal Ascot. I had punched the air when she kicked clear and hyperventilated when her competitors lunged for her on the line. But did that explain this heavy dread? Our girl had won, hadn't she?

And then it hit me: I'd stayed up to watch a horse race because I couldn't sleep, and I couldn't sleep because the Dogs got a beating. And my sleeping superpowers desert me when the Dogs get a beating.

'We need to get an early lead, because once the beers kick in after half time it could all go downhill.'
Anonymous Rockdog

I still haven't quite worked out the vibe of the Reclink Community Cup. It's all over the place, in the best possible way. If it was an album it would be the Rolling Stones' *Exile on Main Street* – lots of flavours.

My role as assistant coach to Paul Kelly was pretty vague. At some point I was going to say a few words before the game – they were my instructions. My moment came early in the day as the whole team took what might be described as a ceremonial walk out to the middle of the ground.

I spoke about things I would speak about to my Bulldog teammates. That the game is about more than spectacular goals and screaming high marks. It has to be about more. If there is a spiritual side to footy, it's a simple bond between teammates that comes from helping each other.

As we walked off the ground, our cheeky half-forward, 'Coops', sidled up next to me and said, 'That's where you're wrong – it's all about the speccies and the goals!'

Clearly, I had some work to do.

I spent the next little while leaning against the wall and just observing the mood of the room. It was futile, because the mood could swing wildly from player to player and moment to moment. The Rockdogs were minutes away from taking to the field to play a game I have played most weeks for 13 years, but it felt like another world.

In the space of a few minutes, three people spoke and the group came together to listen; it was very quiet. The first two speakers I know simply as 'Ox' and 'Jonesy'. Both men spoke about what the day meant to them and what it meant to be a Rockdog. They talked about playing in memory of those who weren't there. It was something I felt privileged to witness.

At this point it was Coach Kelly's turn to speak, and the group huddled close. To say Kelly has a way with words is the kind of understatement that can give you nausea, but to stand shoulder to shoulder with him as he gave his Rockdogs a last little piece of advice is something that will stay with me forever.

In his own delicate way, he brought the team back to itself. 'We are the only team in the world comprised totally of musicians,' he said. 'Just like being in a band, we can't make that big, beautiful noise we want to make on our own – we need our mates.'

In the short time I'd spent with Paul and the Rockdogs, he often spoke about the basics, how talking to your teammates was so important; that's how you become a team – when everyone feels a part of it. What he said next I've never before heard said in a football context.

I'm paraphrasing, but what I remember him saying is this: 'We need the Megahertz. They are our dance partners. We need to play the Rockdog way, which is tough but fair. Let's lead them on a merry dance.'

Never before had I heard anyone say that they 'need' their

opposition, but if it's to be a proper contest, you do, and they need you. In this context, we let the Brisbane Lions down last week. I'd hate to do the same to the Bombers.

28 June 2012

WHEN THE WINNING GETS TOUGH, KEEP ON RUNNING

'It's supposed to be hard. If it wasn't hard everyone would do it.
The hard . . . is what makes it great.'
Tom Hanks, *A League of their Own*

I've fallen in love with running again. It happened a few weeks ago when I took off around Princes Park. I ran, on my own, just to run, and it was quite beautiful. I hadn't run for the pure joy of it for years. I'd missed it.

For the past 12 or 13 years, running has been a vehicle for my work. A way for me to chase opponents or get away from them. Often against the clock, and always against myself, running has been almost a daily routine of getting fitter, stronger and tougher, both in body and in mind. The modern game is open more than ever to footballers of all shapes and size, with one condition: you have to be able to run.

It so happened that a week after my jaunt around the park I received a book as a birthday gift. It's called *Born to Run*, and Christopher McDougall's words have fanned the flames of an old flame – running. The book explores the mysterious and fascinating world of 'ultra runners' – specifically, an ancient Mexican tribe from the Copper Canyon called the Tarahumara.

The Tarahumara have a few names but one bestowed on them by the West is 'the running people'. For thousands of years these men and women have run for days on end for the simple joy it brings them. Not for money, not for sponsorship, not even for a medal or ribbon. They run because it makes them happy. Seemingly, they run to find inner peace.

When I was a kid, if I wasn't on my bike I was on my feet. One of the things that my siblings and I used to love doing at our cousins' place in Dandenong was to knock on people's doors and run off. We thought it was the sport of kings. (I now know that driving with your car on empty is the true sport of kings.) I was pretty fast for a little tacker and would win the odd running race, but I saved my fastest time for when we knocked on the wrong door and a German shepherd leapt out of the front yard and chased me all the way home. On that night, I would've run an A-qualifier and trumped both Steve Solomon and John Steffensen for the 400-metre dash.

One of the intriguing things about *Born to Run* is its exploration of the difficulties all runners are confronted with and challenged to overcome. Ultra runners are the extreme, running competitively over an entire day, but even your weekend plodder has hurdles laid out in front of them, whether it's the burning in the lungs or the aching fatigue of the mind. Everyone's will to go on is tested.

Over the years I've been privileged to listen to some amazing athletes talk about their experiences. I remember vividly one in particular, an Olympic runner, telling our playing group back 2001: 'In terms of my sport, I made it to the penthouse, right to the top. I can honestly say that I never once took the easy option.'

Most of the players in the room thought that was pretty amazing, and what an inspiration it was. I was in the minority – I thought it was total garbage. He gave the impression he was indestructible. I don't think I believed him. Who can relate to that kind of perfection?

Years later, the former Olympic swimmer Mark Spitz spoke to us, and he had a slightly different take. He spoke about the days when he wasn't quite mentally there for the battle that lay ahead. He knew that, to win, he had to endure huge pain. He judged himself not on the days that he swam with ease and grace, but on those days when he stood on the blocks and had to find something that he wasn't sure was there. Now that is deserving of the penthouse.

I'll share with you one last story, and it comes from a young boy called Jacob Mibus. I first met Jacob four and a half years ago, shortly after he lost his foot from the ankle down in a horrible accident. Through some mutual friends I was asked to visit him in the Royal Children's Hospital (Jacob is a passionate little Bulldogs supporter), and I've kept in touch with the Mibus clan ever since.

In the middle of a pretty gloomy week at the Kennel, Jacob's parents texted me to say he had just won the state championship for cross-country in his division. They stopped in on their way home to Dunkeld and I got to shake the hand of our state's newest champion.

Jacob lost a foot and he keeps going, keeps running. The Bulldogs have lost a few games and maybe a bit of our dignity. But we must keep running.

19 July 2012

FOOTY LIFE – I'M SOAKING IN IT

Having shared a cab ride home from the city one night with a soon-to-be-famous opposition footballer, I bumped into him again a few months later in a Torquay video shop. We'd built up some rapport (or so I thought) in that late-night journey home, but it soon became pretty clear that this future super-star had no idea who I was. 'Are you down here for schoolies?' he asked me.

It was in that instant that I knew that he had no idea who I was. My heart both sank and leapt at once, and the little voice in my head whispered, 'Back away, back away!' Apparently, the Abletts have been known to forget the odd name or two.

It's a funny dance when footballers bump into each other away from the field of play and exchange pleasantries and small talk. It's odd because most of the time you know of each other but really don't know each other very well at all. At other times, like the one in Torquay, it all breaks down into a calamitous comedy.

The St Kilda Sea Baths are a bit of a meeting spot for AFL players, not that we plan it that way a lot of the time. It's a place to heal and cleanse, both physically and mentally; it is a place where you go by yourself, even if you're in a group, if you get what I mean.

The 'Mick' in me likens it a little bit to going to church. Whether it's prayer you're after or the soothing warmth of salted water on your battered limbs, what is important is that you feel able to drop your armour at the door and leave all those little anxieties behind as you look for quiet, warmth and rejuvenation. Which is difficult when you walk into a crowded spa full of opposition players.

Going back a few years, I was in what was almost a hypnotic state as I entered the sea baths. Because it's part of your routine over many weeks, you could almost complete these rituals half-asleep – sometimes you are.

On this particular day, I wandered into the changerooms, derobed, showered and then walked out to the poolside and put my bag down. I was half-submerged in the hydrotherapy pool, up to my waist in water, when I looked up and, to my horror, saw the entire North Melbourne Kangaroos footy team looking at me as they went about their recovery/confession. What to do?

Well, in times like those it's best to pretend this is how you planned things all along, despite the voice in your head screaming, 'Turn around! Get out!' I gave a quick 'high-eyebrow hello' in the general direction of the beefed-up blokes, and waded over to a corner like a discarded lamb from the flock.

I was in my early 20s at the time and hardly sure of myself in the big, tough world of AFL. So I stayed in my corner to sweat it out. After a couple of excruciating minutes, Leigh Colbert walked over and stuck his hand out, and we had what's known as 'the footy chat': 'How's the body holding up? Where's your footy trip headed?'

At some point one of you will ask, 'Who have you got this week?' That's the equivalent to that point in any phone conversation when someone drops the, 'All right then . . .' and you both realise your little chat is over and negotiate your exits.

Life and football life certainly have a way of repeating themselves, and just this week, after attending a funeral in Brighton, my skipper and I thought we might take the chance to swing by our bayside health retreat. Older and perhaps a little wiser than my early 20s self, I knew something was up straight away. The car park was full of Jeeps, and pretty soon a wave of Tigers footballers came spewing out of doorways and out from behind cars in packs of two and three.

Eyebrows were up in the heavens as we quickfire greeted each other. Trent Cotchin even offered me his parking ticket, which had some time left on it. He's impossible not to like (even after he'd taken my Dogs apart two days earlier). A great player, and a gentleman to boot.

As the Jeep'd army headed out the gates, a swarm of Mazdas flew right back in to take their spots and I was reminded of that Kangaroos recovery session of years gone by. Before you knew it, Boydy and I were up to our waists in hot water, fending for ourselves against a spritely pack of Roos, our eyebrows lost in the clouds.

16 August 2012

I FORGET THE WORDS, BUT FOR US THE FAT LADY HAS SUNG

'Like a bat out of hell, looking over the bridge, to the MCG . . .'

Meat Loaf really captured the spirit of football and Melbourne with his classic song 'Leaps and Bounds' at last year's Grand Final, didn't he? That's Meat Loaf, isn't it? Maybe it's a Paul Kelly lyric . . . I can't remember any more. Sure is a good line, though.

I keep second-guessing myself this week; everything feels a bit back to front when the season comes to an early finish. And I haven't even been on the drink yet. Things might get very surreal if we break out the gin . . . How many tears in a bottle of gin, anyway?

It doesn't matter. Finals are what's on everyone's mind and, as a proud Melburnian, who am I to snub the city's favourite festival just because all Bulldog folk feel like a waterlogged ball that no one wants to kick around any more?

Waterlogged or not, that didn't stop my daughter, Frankie, putting on her Bulldogs jumper last Monday as we had lunch as a family at my local Fitzroy watering hole, the Commercial Club

Hotel. She's proud of her Dogs, as loyal as they come, but at just two and a half, perhaps she's also a little naive or sheltered to the relevance of ladder positions, finals and all that hoopla.

Usually on a Monday at this time of year, Frankie's dad is huddled around a Bulldogs team poster with darts flying into it amid raucous laughter, jeers, cheers and a few beers. As my little crew sat quietly in the warm sun, tucking into our fish and chips and slow-roasted pork belly, a CCH patron leant over to me and asked: 'Is this what Mad Monday looks like these days?'

You could say we were a long way from the dart board. All footy seasons are unique – some should be celebrated, others mourned, and then there are the seasons that are quickly swept up and put in the dustbin. This is one of those years.

We'll get together as a team and as a club over the coming days and weeks, enjoy each other's company, pay tribute to a couple of retired Dogs. But a celebration is not on the cards.

In some ways next season feels like it has already begun; a post-match debrief from our leader, Brendan McCartney, made that pretty clear. Quite obviously, the Dogs have a lot of ground to make up. I'm sure there'll be a few footy followers keen to remind me of this when we have a chat at various urinals around town over the next little bit. Why do we blokes enjoy a chat at urinals? We do all the dumb things, don't we?

With the house lights fading on the 'Scray and the other teams who pulled up outside the eight, a huge amount of voltage is this weekend surging towards the teams up the top. It's another of footy's great juxtapositions for those whose teams didn't make it – the fact that it's hard to watch and even harder to look the other way.

A few of my brethren and I are heading for Nevada this week for a bit of a holiday. As a bloke who doesn't gamble and sunburns indoors, I should fit right in. I'm already on the look-out for an Irish bar that might play the first round of AFL finals for me. I'm pretty keen to see who can get on a roll – and to see if the Yanks enjoy a chat at a urinal as much as we do.

6 September 2012

2013

SING WHEN YOU'RE WINNING

Sometime in an early '90s winter, the Murphy family took off down the highway from Warragul and headed for the iconic MCG. Our footballing pilgrimages were usually made to the much closer and far more underwhelming Waverley Park. Dad must've really fancied the Tigers' chances.

I can only remember three things from that day. One: the Tigers won, which at the time was like witnessing Halley's Comet. Two: David Cloke kicked a goal from close range into the worksite that would become the Southern Stand at the Punt Road end. Three: the Richmond banner read: 'Winners are grinners and we'll be smiling after this one.'

I can't really explain why that banner has stayed with me all these years, but (as much as the Dogs' cheer squad will hate me for saying so) it's the only one I can remember. Gee, it was good to have a win.

It's okay to say it out loud if your team got a win too. In the 'process'-driven world of AFL football, where everyone is looking for 'the edge', it doesn't hurt to take a few moments with your comrades or brethren and enjoy the end result.

In years gone by, players would enjoy a win by getting on the drink for a few days. Slowly but surely the enjoyment of a win has receded like the polar icecaps. For today's crop of players, the idea of having a quiet beer in the social rooms with the opposition after a game is like hearing old ghost stories. It's hard to imagine it happening, but it's also hard to imagine life getting any better than that. Progress isn't always for the best.

Sadly, it could be getting even worse. 'The ten minutes after a win are bliss' is common footy blather, but has more recently been pared down to 'those five minutes after a win are great'. Oh dear. Some coaches now tell us that 'you have to move on from a win straight away'.

Blimey. Give it another year and we'll be cutting the last verses of our theme song because it's what other sides are doing. Sing that extra verse and you could potentially open yourself up to the most dreaded of sins: 'They've got ahead of themselves.'

We haven't got carried away out at Footscray. The dark days and sleepless nights of last year are still very fresh in our minds, and we now begin the slow crawl into the light.

Since Brendan McCartney came on board, he's been trying to paint a picture. At times, we've been asked to paint a picture of our own, of how we want to play to our members and the wider public, through the media. But for the most part we've been trying to paint a picture, sculpt a stone or compose a tune of how we want to play. Hours upon hours of work have been put in, teaching, coaching, practising, reviewing, arguing and cajoling each other to shape a game of football the way we want it to be.

We have a young group. It takes time and we're not there yet, but last week was the clearest picture we've had yet. You can run through it a million times on the track and on a video screen, but until the players can do it for themselves on match day, true belief can linger just out of reach.

Confidence is a funny thing, and in football it gets spoken of a lot. Most players grapple with the mystery of how to find it, and the perennial question, 'Where did it go?' Something that's of more relevance, I believe, is a player's and a team's self-esteem. It is relevant for every team, for every athlete in the world.

Positive-parenting guru Louise Hart said, 'Self-esteem is as important to our wellbeing as legs are to a table,' and I think she's right. Self-esteem in the modern footballing landscape comes from a player's ability to play his role for the team.

Self-esteem is not gained, as I understand it, from a spectacular mark, a lace-out pass to the full-forward, or a banana goal from the fourth row. Those things are football fairy-floss. Self-esteem comes from whether you were able to produce effort to a level your teammates expect of you. The (full version) theme song is a celebration of that as much as anything else.

That and winning, of course.

4 April 2013

A PAINFUL LOSS, ICY WATERS AND TWO BRICKS

'In the hour of greatest slaughter, the great avenger is being born.'
PAUL KELLY, 'BRADMAN'

The siren goes and everything stops. For a few moments, anyway. There's an energy in the stadium that rises and falls like a wave, but you have none.

You look up at the scoreboard and it doesn't seem real. Hell, the last two hours don't feel real. Walking off the ground to the boos of your own and the cheers of theirs, you get the feeling deep inside your soul that things are about to feel very real indeed. Round 9, 2011: West Coast 26.19 (175) d Western Bulldogs 8.4 (52). You can imagine the flight home. It felt like we'd gone via Denmark.

Anyone who has played footy for a while at any level has been in a side that's been belted. It's just one of those unpleasant certainties of a football life. But there are a few games in a player's career that can leave you shell-shocked.

The 2011 debacle in Perth had the added stink of an ageing playing list and a coach under pressure to keep his job. A footy club is incredible at keeping the rest of the world at arm's length to create a world inside itself, but when defeats break the 100-point barrier, those tensions and attacks from the outside can seep through.

The most uncomfortable thing in the aftermath of our trip to Perth was the silence. The coaching staff, led by 'Rocket' Eade, had decided on a tough love approach that was pretty lean on the 'love'. Our instructions after the game were very clear: 'Come prepared to work, come prepared to hurt.'

Where normally the day after catching the 'red eye' is about treatment, a paddle in the saltwater, a long walk, a massage and hopefully some sleep, we headed to Victoria University for a searching swim session – something in the vicinity of two kilometres. The mood set by our fitness boss, Bill Davoren – and with not a single coach at the pool – added to the growing unease.

We were then sent home with a kicker: be at Port Melbourne beach the next morning, five o'clock, and bring two bricks. The dank smell in the air told me we weren't getting an early start to build a fence. I'm sure all of us closed our eyes that night for a while, but you couldn't call it sleep. My two bricks sat neatly next to my bedroom door, but I felt like I had a dozen in my stomach. That's what shame feels like.

Pre-dawn, the full roster plunged into the icy water off the pier and swam for shore. Cold and shaking, we then stood in a circle with bricks outstretched and said hello to Mr Pain.

For a moment you fight the pain on your own, until the penny drops as to why you're there in the first place. It's about you holding up your bricks to make life easier for the bloke next to you, and him doing the same for you. A footy team at its most basic point.

Though tinged with anger, the voices of our coaches returned to our world and 'encouraged' us not to be the first to let our arms fall. This went on for quite a while.

Our next set of instructions were laid out: meet back at the club in a few hours, and be ready for a football session. The players who didn't go back to bed for an emergency kip gathered for breakfast in a cafe near the pier. It was only toast, coffee and company, but the redemption had begun. As players, we were already leaning on each other, because we only had each other.

Back at the club, guys readied themselves for training as if they were going to war and might not come home. Training was mapped out by a still-seething Rocket. Just before we took to the track, Rocket read out six or seven names and told us they were the blokes who competed. I wasn't one of them. Telling a footballer he's not competitive is to disembowel him. Daniel Cross was in the group of competitors.

The footy session was as brutal as it gets in the modern era of sports science and individually managed training loads. A thumb and a shoulder were dislocated in the 'search' for competitors, but the standout in each drill was a little fella with dreadlocks called Luke Dahlhaus. His competitive spirit shone, and though he was about to make himself known to the rest of the footy world in a few days, on this day he put himself on the internal map.

When I see Luke today, I'm reminded of that line from Paul Kelly's tribute to 'The Don'. The physical purge complete, the next phase was the mechanics. Footy is played with the head and the heart – we'd dealt with the heart, now it was time for the duality of why we do the things we do when the pressure comes. How your actions affect your teammates around you.

Watching the game tape wasn't pretty, but with Rocket in full swing something rather strange happened. The fire alarm went off, a heaving siren with the warning, 'THIS IS NOT A DRILL!' Rocket tried to yell over the alarm, but it got louder and louder. Even in the depths of a 100-point depression, I thought to myself, 'This will be funny one day.'

The rest of the week was a build. There was still steel in the eyes, but where there had been silence some warmth re-entered our world. Win together, lose together. 'Us against the world' is not just a catchy line but an accurate description of how you feel in times like these.

We lost to the Saints that week too, but every now and then it's not simply about the four points. We were all elevated into the group that included Daniel Cross: competitors. For 200 games he has been a ruthless competitor. We couldn't be prouder of him.

11 April 2013

KEEPING UP
WITH THE KIDS

'Would you like to play football like Dad one day, mate?'

'Um, yeah. But, Dad, do you know what I really want to do? When I grow up I want to catch lizards and frogs!'

This pretty much sums up the level of importance football plays in my young fella Jarvis's world. He's aware of football, he knows his dad plays and so do plenty of Dad's friends who come by the house. He's seen them on TV, he's got his Dogs jumper with number two on the back, and he likes the theme song when Dad sings it in the car (especially the trumpet solo).

But beyond that, there is a fogginess to it all. His obsessions lie elsewhere. He's only five years old, after all.

His little sister, Frankie, is only three, but she has a bit more clarity: 'Dad, you should play for the Tigers. The Tigers are the best. The Tigers winned.'

This outburst would have been fine in the family kitchen, but little Frankie announced her new footy leanings at the Bulldogs' post-match function straight after the loss to the

Tigers – within earshot of the senior coach! It was like a grenade going off.

Jarvis started primary school this year, and last week was the annual footy day. Jarvis's mum and I were curious as to what – if any – effect this would have on our amphibian-loving little boy.

We didn't get off to a great start to footy day. In the morning rush we'd forgotten his footy jumper and had to make a quick dash back home. This had shades of 1995 about it, when Geelong's Shayne Breuer came to our high school and I'd forgotten my footy kit. Luckily, my mum was a teacher at the school and was able to dash home to get it for me. Mums . . . bless 'em.

Once we'd gotten Jarvis in his red, white and blue, the school had an assembly where each kid got to run around the group, high-fiving as they went. The message from above was a clear one: the day was about cheering and encouraging, getting into the spirit of things, no matter what team colours you wore, or even if you didn't have any colours on show. Some people at the grown-ups' footy could learn a lot from that little assembly.

It was great to see plenty of old Fitzroy jumpers in the playground. I felt unexpected pangs of pride and admiration for these kids and their folks as they joined in with their classmates.

There weren't too many other Bulldog jumpers to be found – in fact, only Jarvis and two others. They'd need to stick together, which kind of comes with the colours. This was going to be interesting. I want my boy to grow up with the freedom of choice, to lead his own life, with one exception: that he barracks for the Dogs. A rogue Essendon soft toy in the crib as a newborn is one thing (easily removed, too) but the pressure of peers is a formidable one to resist.

My anxiety was heightened by the horrifying news that some Carlton players were coming to the school that day for a footy clinic. Last year it was Chris Judd. Oh dear.

For Jarvis's dad, every day is footy day. Most of them I spend trying to keep up with the 'kids' at the Kennel. They're not really kids, though. Jarvis couldn't pick me up and throw me over the fence if he wanted to – but Jake Stringer could.

After another day at the football factory I headed for school pick-up, wondering what kind of day my little mate had at school. Would his loyalty to the Bulldogs have been tested by the appearance of the men in navy blue? What about his mates? I know young Jake barracks for the Cats, but I wasn't sure about Hugo or Axl. I was prepared for the worst.

I waited next to the other mums and dads as the kids sprawled out in all directions, and took some heart that at least he still had his Footscray jumper on.

'Did the footballers come to your class today, mate?'

'No, they only took the Grade Ones and Fours.'

This was a joyous moment for me. 'Who's our team?' I asked Jarvis.

'The Bulldogs, Dad. Don't you know that? But I have two teams . . .'

I almost lost my footing. Then he explained.

'I have two teams – the Bulldogs and the Inverloch/Kong-wak Sea Eagles. That's my cousin Fred's team.'

Order restored, we'd made it through footy day in one piece.

2 May 2013

THE DREAM
THAT NEVER DIES

The Boston Red Sox baseball franchise in the Major League of America is a famous source of both fascination and inspiration for sports lovers all over the world.

Thrust into prominence in the early 20th century through the heroics of a champion team and Babe Ruth's charismatic talent, the Red Sox were the hottest ticket around. Inexplicably, they then traded 'the Babe' to the New York Yankees, where he won even more championships and established the Yankees as the powerhouse franchise of the world. They remain so to this day, and the 'Curse of the Bambino' was born.

Between 1946 and 2004 the Red Sox didn't win a single pennant, despite coming painfully close a few times. That all changed when, 0–3 down in the best-of-seven American League Championships Series (against the Yankees, of course), the Red Sox fought their way back to claim the title, rid themselves of the curse and etch their names into sporting folklore for ever.

ESPN made a documentary on this incredible story simply

titled *Four Days in October*. About four weeks ago I sat down
to watch it, and it nearly ripped me in half.

In the final stages of the World Series, with victory a mere
formality, the documentary makers were able to capture the
emotions of the Red Sox players and fans. Generations upon
generations of broken hearts came together to cry, to cheer,
to hold one another close and live in the world of their dreams.
As I sat watching, I couldn't help but draw the obvious com-
parisons to me and my Bulldogs.

Watching the jubilation in the Red Sox dressing room, I
was struck dumb to consider the possibility that I could be
watching the Bulldogs claim our 'pennant' one day and, like
the faces on the screen in front of me, I wouldn't recognise
them, not in the way I recognise my teammates now. It was a
twist of the blade in my stomach, and I knew in an instant I
had not completely mourned my faded chance.

That might sound like snivelling jealousy to some, but jealousy lurks in all of us, whether we're proud of it or not. After
the 2011 Grand Final the TV cameras captured Joel Selwood
and Tom Hawkins running to each other and embracing seconds after the final siren. You could see on their faces the joy
of two mates bound together forever in glory.

I had to leave the room when I saw that. It's not a simple
cry of 'Why not me?' .– it's 'Why couldn't that be me and Gia?
Me and Boydy? Me and Huddo? Crossy and Boydy?'

The thing that has surprised me about this mourning is it
has hit me in stages. I think I've dealt with it and then, boom!
I can't speak for my older teammates or players from other
teams, but I suspect it would be true for them, too. In 2009,
when we missed out on a Grand Final by a kick, we all slumped

against the wall of the changerooms and could do little more than cry for one another. Maybe that was our chance.

In 2010 we made it to the Preliminary Final again, but there were times that year when I thought to myself that we weren't travelling as well as we had been before, and maybe our window was beginning to close. But you brush it off and push on. Then the dark clouds gathered for real in 2011 and no longer were we able to run teams off their legs – now we were being put to the sword. No finals, coach gone, window slams shut. So what do you do?

There are choices. Do you jump ship? If ever there was a time, it's probably now. Or do you stay? You can only stay if you have absolute clarity on exactly why that is – and it is this: to help. With whatever you've got left in your head, your legs or your heart, you have to give that to Luke Dahlhaus, Jordan Roughead, Ryan Griffen. To Mitch Wallis and Tom Liberatore. To Liam Jones and Ayce Cordy. To your teammates who might yet have their Red Sox moment. The torch of the dream still burns in them – even in our current plight, it burns. They have time left to do it. There will be the odd pinch of grief now and again for me and the older ones. It will feel like a hole in our hearts but maybe that's just part of growing up.

Two weeks ago a friend gave me a Chicago Cubs baseball cap. I've chosen them as my new team – I wonder if other Bulldog supporters seek out success-starved clubs in other codes too? My Cubs cap is my invite to their inevitable pennant party, just as a Bulldogs membership is a name on the door at Footscray Town Hall on that one day when the Dogs bring home the pennant. I may not know their faces, but all of us will be living out our dreams.

For now, all we can do is help each other get there, one piece at a time. Gold Coast this Saturday is the next little piece.

16 May 2013

HEROIC GESTURES
AND MEN OF ACTION

'You guys took a lot of big hits out there tonight.'
JOHN VAN GRONINGEN

I drove out to Southern Cross Grammar in the western suburbs this week with my teammate Jarrad Grant, for a reading
session with some Grade Prep children. This was unusual;
generally we're asked to take footy clinics and talk about
healthy eating. I'm an expert on the food pyramid.

I told the little kids who were sat cross-legged on the floor
that I had a son who was in Grade Prep too. This was a mistake, because for the next two minutes they all looked around
the room to see if he was sitting among them. To clear up con-
fusion and regain control of my class, I started to read, and a
hushed silence fell over them.

Marngrook: The Long Ago Story of Aussie Rules begins with
one of the elders, Wawi, coming across a possum, which he
kills, skins, then ties up with rubbery tendon and stuffs with
emu feathers to make the very first marngrook (or football).
Wawi gives the ball to the little ones, including Jaara. After
taking off with the marngrook, young Jaara kicks it into the

bush and promptly gets lost. He then finds himself in a mini coming-of-age tale.

It's hard work getting Prep kids to sit together and face the same direction, let alone have them carried away on the same story for too long. But that's what the power of this story did for them – and for me, too.

My very first marngrook jumper was that of the Warragul Colts and I had the number seven on the back. I was a Tigers supporter but this was my tribute to Nicky Winmar. He was one of my heroes. The dashing runs, the high marking, the grace. He had it all.

Strangely enough, my first day at the Kennel in late 1999 was Nicky's last. As Mum and Dad drove us home to Warragul, and I keenly inspected my new Bulldogs training gear, the announcement came over the radio that 'Winmar hadn't shown for day one of pre-season and would not be playing on'.

This week it's the AFL's Indigenous Round, as we pay tribute to the Indigenous culture of footy, and also reflect on the iconic photograph of Nicky at Victoria Park. And the Bulldogs play the Saints – Nicky's two AFL clubs.

My mate Paddy is a St Kilda supporter and runs a proper pub in Fitzroy. Hanging on the wall in the main bar is that photo of Nicky Winmar defiantly pointing to his stomach. The power of that photo tells you a lot about the pub and a lot about Paddy.

At AFL House there is a huge mural in the foyer with a montage of images capturing the spirit of footy. The image that jumps out at me is Nicky's. Like at the front bar of my local, it lays down a standard of behaviour, a set of values, an ambition for the future.

John Van Groningen grew up in California but found his way to Australia and was drawn to the outback. John was many things to many people, but among his numerous accomplishments he was the founder of the Red Dust charity, which takes sporting role models to Indigenous communities. John was also the chaplain at the Western Bulldogs for the best part of a decade.

On a trip to Darwin last year I sat by the pool with John and we chatted about real things – life, death, family, love, community. He told me of his plans for the future, and how he was about to embark on a major study that would send him to the remote communities of Australia. In his work with Red Dust, John would take role models from different fields, many from sport, and embark on these epic trips into the desert. This study he was embarking on had a different bent, though.

What John told me that day will stay with me forever. He said that 'people dream in their first language'. John's hope was that with his study he could go into the Indigenous communities of the Northern Territory and find out what kids in those communities really wanted to be, what they dreamt of becoming.

Tragically, in the months after our conversation, John became very ill. Just before Christmas he died.

When John and I talked about upcoming trips to the Tiwi or Alice, I'd make tentative plans to take my family up into the communities. But there was always a tinge of, 'Yeah, one day I'll get up there with Justine and the kids . . . one day.'

Driving home from John's funeral, I was overwhelmed with sadness and guilt at never going on one of those trips. My wife reminded me that the door wasn't closed, and that we owed it to John to get up there. These things are a bit like a developing team and the traps that lurk: 'One day we'll be a good side . . . yeah, one day.'

At some point you have to make the decision to just go.

23 May 2013

FROM SPACE TO BREATHE TO SPACE TO KICK

It may look confusing to those watching at home, but there is often method in what appears to be madness on the field. This is the part of modern football that doesn't translate very well to television. Let's paint the picture, shall we?

The game has been frenetic, and as players from both teams heave with lungs expanding and contracting, someone takes a mark. The game slows, almost to a stop. One player has the ball in his hand, in his control. He is hemmed in by the boundary line on one side and his opponent straight ahead, who is keeping guard on the mark. The player with the ball is standing on centre wing. Now the defensive structures (everyone's favourite) are quickly forming in front of him; his team's forward half begins to fill up like Piccadilly Circus at peak hour. Meanwhile, the other half of the ground empties.

If you're watching at home, you can't really tell what's happening. Why is such a skilful footballer looking down the field with a look of concern and frustration on his face? The cameras capture the eyes of the panicked player darting all over the place, but before long he finds what he's looking for. And you can't believe it.

'Backwards? You went backwards *and* sideways!' comes the cry from a thousand lounge rooms. 'What's wrong with kicking the bloody thing long down the middle! There's 18 of you blokes out there!'

This little scenario is something modern players are faced with over and over again. But no matter how many times you've rehearsed, when it happens on game day there will always be some little nuance that makes it unique. Doesn't that just capture footy? You've seen it all a million times, but you've never seen it like this!

The biggest difference in this scenario for the supporter at home compared with the players on the ground or the spectator sitting on level two is an appreciation of the number of opposition players who have swarmed into the area of the most direct route to goal. If the player with the ball kicks it straight down the line, he's likely kicking it to an outnumbered situation and his team will lose possession.

With no free players available in front of you, the mission now becomes to find your free players in space, and very likely they will be found sideways and maybe even slightly backwards. Breathe. This is a good thing. Your team is trying to get the ball to the other side of the ground so that it can then move forward with purpose, and kick it to the forwards who have space to lead into.

Like every game of the year, this exact scenario played out between the Saints and the Dogs on Saturday. True to form, it was like no other. On Saturday night it was Dale Morris with the ball, and St Kilda quickly swarmed to the dangerous part of the ground. Morris turned sideways and kicked backwards, to groans. I just happened to be the player on the other end in space, and while I was getting into position I noticed my opponent was Ben McEvoy, all 200 centimetres of him.

As the ball came in my direction I'd already decided I was going to try to run around him. While I was packing my bags for the short trip around McEvoy, the ball slipped through my legs and I had to scamper back. In an instant the scenario was turned on its head; I felt in my bones that it was now going to be a big moment in the game.

Big bloke versus little bloke in a game of speed . . . even some of the Dogs supporters were probably hoping McEvoy would catch me. Fear makes for good fuel, and with it I tried to get around the man mountain in search of the green fields of Ireland (or Etihad, as it was). A quick turn and shimmy and I thought I was home free, but then came a moment that will stay with me until the day I die. McEvoy's presence swallowed me up, and his hand touched down on my back. He'd run me down.

I could feel the excitement and dread of 30,000 people run through my legs, and I was about to be the villain. Big guy who never gives up catches the cocky little smartarse, and the game turns on its head. I've probably cost my club the game, I thought. For some reason I thought it would be a good idea to bounce the ball out in front and try for a higher gear. Somehow it worked.

The moment of pure terror passed, and the field opened up. I picked a spot and kicked it as far as I could. Ryan Griffen took the mark and kicked a goal.

There was plenty of luck involved, and I did nearly cost my boys the game, but we were due a bit of good fortune. Every set play has its nuance. This time it was a mismatch and a fumble.

30 May 2013

THE 'G FORCES
STILL DRAW US IN

At least once a year I like to watch footy from the outer as a neutral spectator. It's a very useful learning tool for a league footballer to watch a game as a punter, but it's not why I go. For me, it fills in a blind spot, giving me a better picture of what the game is all about.

I've done it for a few years now, an annual pilgrimage to the MCG. I call up a mate, put my duffle coat on and soak up the Melbourne experience.

Last week I went with an old mate of mine, Nigel – he's a Dogs supporter, just like me. I went along looking for a close game. Nigel was barracking against Essendon supporters.

We headed out my front door at 6.30 sharp and briskly walked the short journey to the tram stop, but there was no tram to be seen. 'Best we wait inside the pub until the next one gets here,' we thought in unspoken unison.

We ordered a couple of Coopers pots and I just gazed at mine for a little while, savouring its majestic amber beauty.

It'd been a while. With a fire hissing and popping in the corner of the small front bar, and the chatty hum of the locals filling the room, we managed to miss the next four trams. We stayed so long we were asked to draw the raffle. We'd been taken in, it seemed, and we felt right at home.

Eventually, we headed up Nicholson Street towards the city with our tram bumping and swaying all the way; I couldn't help but marvel at a young lady who had nerves of steel as she applied eyeliner with the sharpest of black pencils. I wondered if the Blues' and Bombers' players were prepared to risk their eyeballs to get their desired result in front of 80,000 people.

As our tram shunted to a stop, I got to enjoy my favourite walk of the year, joining the thousands of pilgrims on the march through Fitzroy Gardens towards the mighty MCG. You don't have to go far these days to hear people talking about how much footy has changed, how it's a business now and how it's all gone a bit too corporate. That may be true in part, but as I wormed my way through the masses of support-ers and got my first glimpse of the 'G, I couldn't help but feel that we still have enough right about this game. Like a pot of Coopers, that patch of grass under the lights on a Friday has a beauty that leaves you with a sense of wonder every time.

Going to the footy doesn't feel that different to when I followed my dad through the crowds on a hundred Saturday afternoons as a kid. The excitement is still there, the anticipa-tion, the tribal nature of footy.

One game a year in the outer is what you might call a small sample size, but something that has changed since those hal-cyon days near the Tigers cheer squad in 1995 is the banter in the crowd. Then, there always seemed to be some punter willing to entertain those around him as the play unfolded – they were often theatrical exclamations, witty, self-deprecating and always funny.

If you were lucky, you'd get a couple of barrackers from opposing teams (usually blokes) who would converse to one another via the play on the field. I can't remember ever having my ears covered by Mum or Dad, nor can I remember being shocked by anything vulgar.

Maybe it's just the familiar warmth of the nostalgia blanket, but I don't hear any of that in the outer these days. What I heard as a kid was entertainment, a performance that had a generosity to it. On my small sample, I hear self-indulgence, bitterness and venomous criticism – even towards members of our own tribes.

Thankfully, at least I didn't hear anything remotely like the recent racial atrocities that have scarred the game. The middle-aged father of three who yelled out for a 'Peter Riccardi and coke!' in the mid-'90s is still out there, I assume. I miss him.

The game between the Blues and the Bombers took a while to get going. Not until the contest got close in the last quarter did I lose myself in it. Jarrad Waite was jumping like a man who knew he could jump higher than the rest and wanted to do it as often as he could, and his seven goals were almost enough to drag the Blues over the line.

The Bombers held the joker in the pack, though. In the NAB Cup this year I was manned up by Jake Carlisle, and because he was so tall I thought that if I kept moving I should be able to get off him. But I never did. He's a beauty.

His second half was extraordinary in both its class and its variety. He had presence of mind up forward – and then, in the dying moments when a hero was needed, he showed all the nerve of the girl on the tram to risk it all for his team.

The walk out of a game at the MCG is a lot less poetic than the walk in, but I was faring a bit better than Nigel, who was surrounded by joyous Bombers fans. In search of one last Coopers, we walked a couple of miles in the Melbourne drizzle; as Rockdogs coach Paul Kelly sings, we could've walked ten more.

The Bulldogs are back on deck this week against everyone's favourites, the Magpies. My next Coopers pot might be a while away, but like the next pilgrimage to the MCG outer, it'll be worth the wait.

13 June 2013

SAVOURING TIME AND THE FOSSIL

A shock loss, a harrowing defeat, an honourable loss, a devastating loss, a gritty win, a brave victory, a come-from-behind win, and occasionally 'Phew, we won'. There are as many ways to win or lose a game as there are games in a season.

My roommate for our Canberra road trip last Saturday was, as usual, Daniel Giansiracusa. Or, as he's more affectionately known at the Kennel these days, 'the Fossil'. Or 'Foss' or 'Pip' or 'Gia'. Come to think of it, I have at least six other names for him that I've used over the years. Most of them pointless, all of them wonderful in their stupidity.

Foss usually drives me to the airport when we travel because he likes to be in charge and in control, and I like to absolve all responsibility. It seems to work. After our light Friday-morning training session at the Whitten Oval, we ducked around the corner to the Footscray Milking Station to break some bread and shoot the breeze. As always, we talk about footy and our families, our loves, our worries. Normal stuff, the best stuff.

This year we've had another guest sit with us, one who never orders from the menu. Quite simply, Time. Our time left together as a travelling pair in a pack of Dogs. Footscray Bulldogs, to be more precise.

In all likelihood, this will be the Fossil's last year and, as we left the cafe with coffees in hand for another drive out to the airport, he remarked that there were only three more road trips left for the season. A few moments of silence fell softly upon us.

'I'll miss our trips away,' I said, looking out the window.

'Me too,' said Foss. He's always been a good finisher.

The end of the road, the final curtain, whatever you want to call it, is often associated or at least tinged with sadness, but I didn't get that feeling in the car. Just an overwhelming sense of thanks. How lucky we've been to play this long together, and how lucky we still are to run out with the boys every week.

By the time our plane touched down in Canberra, notions of curtain calls and Father Time were all but gone. With a game less than 24 hours away, each player goes into his own routine, applying each piece of mental and physical armour he will need to combat the enemy the next day.

It's still the most difficult thing about playing footy at the elite level, I think, the idea of putting your own reputation and the reputation of your club on the line every time you run through the banner. It's the single thing that simultaneously breaks you down over time and also puts air in your tyres.

As is customary, we arose early on Saturday morning, game day, at our team hotel. Foss and I pottered about our room, manoeuvring between our private business and side-stepping each other as we got dressed, in silence, with the grace and familiarity of ballroom dancers. There's always an intriguing tension on game day, and it doesn't fade with age or experience.

I think it would be reasonable to assume that there was an edginess to our entire travelling party last week. We'd been beaten by the recently tormented Demons a week earlier, and now we were facing the young bloods of the competition, Greater Western Sydney, on neutral ground. Despite their own disappointing win-loss record this year, I'm sure the young Giants would've smelt blood. Often, sides at the lower end of the ladder save their best for opponents alongside them. All clubs are desperate for wins. It was always going to be a willing contest.

The game itself never rose to any great heights, but the endeavour and spirit of both sides, combined with the blustery wind, kept things tight all day. My old mate Foss didn't seem his usual self in the first half, and we could've done with a couple of his trademark goals. But we hung in there as a group. As did the Giants.

When it came time to stand up in the last quarter, our boys did, and though it wasn't pretty, we escaped with an 'ugly win'. We couldn't care less about how pretty they are. When the time came for the Fossil to put his stamp on the game, he did. He's always been a good finisher. He also happens to be much more than that.

In the rooms afterwards, we sang our tribal hymn with great gusto. The song is a symbolic release of players taking off their emotional armour – or it is to me, anyway. Just outside the circle and in my line of vision, I could see Time once more. Crushing defeats, heartbreaking losses, ugly wins, pretty wins. In the end, what matters is who you got to share them with.

11 July 2013

DOGGED DEBUT LAUNCHES A CAREER

Everyone remembers his first game of league footy. Mine was in 2000, against a Carlton side that had won 14 games in a row. I was part of a Bulldogs team that was hit hard by injuries, hence my inclusion. I was a boy. Still at high school and with a hulking 68-kilogram frame, I had only recently produced armpit hair.

Terry Wallace had announced to the playing group at training that I would be making my debut, and from that moment I think I knew life would never be the same. As I sat in my Year 12 classes at Footscray City College, I was somewhere else. My dedication to my studies had always been a little 'mixed', but once I got word that I'd be getting a game for the Bulldogs, I was away. Looking out to the horizon from the classroom window, I felt like no one could touch me. I was bouncing on a wave.

The surge carried me all the way to Optus Oval on Saturday, 15 July 2000. I remember being so nervous when I got to the ground, and really worried in the on-field warm-up that I wouldn't be able to kick the ball to my teammate in the most basic of lane work drills. The Carlton cheer squad had gathered behind the goals where we were warming up, and they seemed so loud. Everything felt new.

As we gathered in the doorway that led out onto the field, the intensity among our group took me aback. These mild-mannered blokes who had welcomed me into their team seven months earlier were now geeing each other up, to the point where a few of them were pushing and shoving. I actually thought for a second that Jose Romero and Simon Garlick were having a fight. This never happened in junior football.

After seeing my teammates nearly kill each other, I was half-expecting to see chariots and lions waiting for us on the field. Instead, we were greeted by a glorious Melbourne afternoon bathed in sunshine, and the loudest, most hostile crowd noise I'd ever known. My feet never touched the ground.

Fourteen seasons on from that day, the words our captain, Scott Wynd, had spoken as we huddled close one last time before the first bounce are still gin-clear in my mind. 'These are the kinds of wins that we'll talk about one day if we bump into each other on the street.' He was only my skipper for one year, just three games, but he left a big impression.

Evidence of how much the game has changed since that day came in the first 50 minutes – throughout which I sat on the bench and did not move. When finally the call came, Matthew Croft soon took a strong mark and went out of his way to give me a handball, and I kicked the ball as far as I could. I was away and bouncing on that wave again.

Whatever Jose and Garlo were up to before the game must

have worked, because they were both killing it. Garlo would end up kicking six goals in a career-best performance.

I was playing on the wing and my opponent was Matthew Lappin. I think he enjoyed having a rare weight advantage, because it seemed like every time there was a ball-up around the ground he would punch me in the guts. I kept thinking to myself, 'Lappin is going to get six weeks when they review this game.' I never punched him back. No charges were laid. It's fair to say I was a little naive back then.

Despite our undermanned team being rank underdogs, we were neck and neck with the Kouta-led Blues deep into the last quarter, and our skipper's prophecy was beginning to become a real possibility. With a few minutes left, I escaped the clutches of my sparring partner and drifted forward, where the ball spilt in my direction.

Suddenly I found myself in a lot of space. I looked up and had a single thought: kick a goal. With each step closer, I could feel the Bulldog faithful lift behind me, and I just knew I was going to put us in front.

As the ball left my boot I looked up, and I remember thinking, *That has to be the ugliest kick to go through for a goal in the history of the game.* I didn't care, nor did the faithful – we were all on that wave again.

Occasionally, Bulldogs supporters remind me that I kicked the winning goal that day. I never feel the need to tell them that, in fact, Carlton kicked a goal straight after mine and then Trent Bartlett got a dodgy free kick and slotted the winner for the Dogs. I don't want to stop the flow of good conversation with frivolous details.

I have a photo at home from that day. I'm sitting on the

changeroom floor with teammates Rohan Smith, Brad Johnson and the hero of the day, Simon Garlick. The photo is taken at the exact moment I'm retelling the story of my first goal, complete with hand gestures to describe the rank, floating spin of the ball.

So much about this game has changed since that glorious afternoon. Thankfully, some things will always stay the same. Beating Carlton is still one of the better ways to spend a Saturday.

With all of this season's froth and bubble, it's important to remember that our game can still be about riding the wave of your team, sharing a yarn with your teammates, and dreaming that the next win might one day be worth stopping an old teammate in the street to reminisce over.

15 August 2013

WHEN POLLIES JOIN FOOTY'S FANTASY LEAGUE

'There's more politics in football than there is in politics.'

In a football season where there's been more saga than screamer, it's fitting that the federal election is now also jockeying for our attention. It's been said the two are inextricably linked. The fight for premiership points and the desperation for popularity votes is the name of the game.

But what if these two battles became one? What would it look like? In this year's Fantasy Football League we get to have a look at a team of current and former 'pollies' – or, as my mate Joe calls them, 'lying bastards'.

The Canberra Promises are on the eve of their big clash against the Disinterested Voters. We'll give you the starting 22 and take you inside the dressing rooms of the Promises for all the thrills and spills of the FFL, pollies style.

Coach, Gough Whitlam: Is to the FFL what Leigh Matthews is to the AFL. His word is final. With a handful of red dirt slipping through his fingers, his every action holds weight, history and finality.

President, Quentin Bryce: 'The General' has sworn in more faces than Ray 'Slug' Jordon. Runs a tight ship.

John Howard (c): Crossed codes from cricket, where he was a highly regarded spin bowler. Though conservative with ball in hand, he has been a model of consistency for the Promises over many years. Has still managed to hold off his deputies' advances on the top job in what was dubbed the 'Malthouse/ Buckley Agreement' by a cheeky national media.

Peter Costello (vc): Runner-up in last year's best-and-fairest to Howard (again). Destined to play second fiddle again this year.

Kim Beazley: Returning to team after the dreaded avuncular fracture to his right foot. Might have lost a yard without a pre-season behind him. It could be past him.

Kevin Rudd: After breaking some ribs (his own) in friendly fire last season, he's been dishing out stab passes ever since, most of them to fellow flanker Julia Gillard. Fans survey is confusing – popular one day, on the nose the next. Mixed reception in the locker room too, but remains a constant on the duffle coats of diehards.

Bob Hawke: First picked, and first to book his own flights for this year's footy trip. Everything about this veteran back pocket just screams, 'Yes!' Did his bit for ticket sales when he proclaimed at the jumper presentation that 'anyone who doesn't show up for Round One is a bum'.

Julia Gillard: 'Bluey' was recruited from Altona via a stint as full-forward for the Footscray Bulldogs. Has had a horror run of late, but we remain optimistic about her future and legacy.

Bob Brown: If Royce Hart was Tassie's goal-kicking machine, Brown is its goal-assist machine. Plays for the greater good.

Tony Abbott: Runs all morning and plays in shorts that would make Warwick Capper blush. The main stopper. Critics say he's clueless when it comes to a game plan, but an insider says he looks set for the big job on 'Boats', an opponent nobody can tackle.

Pauline Hanson: Received a 'please explain' from FFL head-quarters after a no-show for multicultural round. Has rebounded strongly on the stats sheet after a bad case of the second-year blues. Divides opinion, not just among redheads.

Mark Latham: Spirited defender who is prone to the odd brain fade. Took all before him as a youngster before falling in a heap when the game was there to be won. Forgotten man of the FFL landscape.

Mal Meninga: Bright career was cut short on debut. Was sighted at training last week, which sparked predictions of a return to the big leagues. A press conference has been called for 9 am tomorrow at FFL house, so who knows?

Bob Katter: An old-fashioned country footballer. Verbose, cocky and just a little bit outrageous, Katter wants the big stage as much as any of his teammates. The shackles are off but the cowboy hat stays on. If he gets near the ball you can bet something will come of it.

Jeff Kennett: Lippy, supposedly reformed character who used to steamroll all in his path and now has a strong interest in player welfare. Picked himself. Literally.

Alexander Downer: Recruited from Adelaide. He'll need to pull his socks up if his pre-season form is anything to go by.

Paul Keating: Charismatic centre half-forward who has the strut and arrogance of the all-time greats. Mixes the flashy with results on the scoreboard. Enjoys the verbal battle. No one was more enthusiastic to bring in a peer feedback program in the off-season. A star.

Kate Ellis: Smart, athletic rookie who looks to be showing some old stagers a clean pair of heels on the training track. All class.

Justin Madden: Lanky ruckman who is under an injury cloud. When pressed about Madden's condition, club doctor John Hewson said, 'Take this cake, for example. If this cake was taxed with GST you'd have to tax the flour, the eggs and the sugar, but not the milk . . .' Pressed, Hewson changed his tune. 'He's fine, he'll play this week.'

And in the tradition of the best leadership challenges, that's it for the Promises, who tried to get to 22 but didn't have the numbers.

22 August 2013

GOING BUSH TO
SWITCH CHANNELS

Some time in the early '90s, my family's trusty television blew up. Well, it didn't blow up kaboom-style, but the picture shrank and continued to shrink until one evening it was just a white dot – like a single shining star on the black backdrop of outer space.

As far as TVs went, it was a sturdy old thing. To change the channel you had to crank the dial like the gears of a tractor. It took us the best part of a year to get another TV, and with a lot of water under the bridge since, I think it was one of the best years for my lot.

Where once the box had been the focal point of entertainment, now we sat down as a five and learnt to play cards, specifically 500. It proved a great vehicle to talk, share and learn about all manner of things, not just the significance of left bowers and what was trumps. Every now and again, it's good to turn the lights off.

In what is now an annual tradition, last weekend I packed

a bag and, along with some of my people, went looking for the peace and quiet of the Australian bush. This most recent trip to the outskirts of Deans Marsh, near Lorne, was the third for our crew, and although the location changes every year and we have had one or two personnel changes, a river of familiarity runs through them. Our travelling party sees each other from time to time all year, but never as a collective, and the routine of building a fire, opening a bottle, eating tender red meat and talking footy is one that fits snugly for all of us.

Our indoor fire and our outside bonfire had just got going as the game between the Tigers and Blues roared to life. There was a gentle sense of warmth leaning to a Tigers win among our group. There is a sense of genuine curiosity about Richmond when it comes to the casual footy observer.

We were watching the game on TV and huddling around the outside fire in shifts, and the Tigers appeared to settle into the game beautifully. When they got five goals up in the third quarter, I left my post for the embers to announce that 'the Tigers are home'. As we migrated back inside the house 15 minutes later, it appeared that they most certainly were not home.

With the footy winding down, the TV was turned off. It never came back on; there were other roads to travel. We limit ourselves to one physical activity a day on these trips, and as the sun fell away from the sky on the first night, we loaded ourselves into the tray of a ute and crept down the hill that ran off into the dense bush looking west. We disembarked and continued west, with the trees quickly swallowing us up. It wasn't long before someone remarked that the landscape was similar to the one that we might associate with Ned Kelly and his gang.

In any gang or team, everyone has a role to play, and our

Ned Kelly historian is also our resident bard, so as we stood in the bush with a glass of plonk in hand, we listened to the story of Ned. The colourful tale had never sounded more fascinating or heroic.

We eventually headed back to the ute; with the back left wheel spinning, we had to get out and push it halfway home.

With a sweat on the brow we made it back to the ranch, and it wasn't long before the conversation turned from Seamus Heaney to football. At last recall, I was locked in a conversation about why and how Dane Swan is such a great player. It was while moving through the kitchen doing my best Swanny shuffle that I realised I'd done the same thing last year. It does go some way in summing up the spirit of this annual pilgrimage.

On our final day a harsh wind ripped through the valley, but sometime in the afternoon it softened and a brilliant sunlight broke through the grey clouds. It stayed like this just long enough for us to have a kick of the footy in our work boots and Blundstones on the edge of a hill.

Some of us kick the footy for a living and some of us haven't kicked it since last year's trip, but I think the moment lifted all our skills to a higher plane. The skies stayed calm just long enough for me to reflect on why a trip like this is so special. It's a final word on the football season just gone, an end to the highs and lows that come with it. But it's also a chance to fall back in love with a game through the eyes and stories of people I find fascinating. That's why, once a year, I like to head for the hills with my gang, and turn off the lights.

12 September 2013

2014

FIFTEEN SEASONS ON, I'M FRETTING ABOUT MY LACES

Personal milestones are, if nothing else, simply a marker of time. As footballers we treasure these markers, think of them as sacred in their own way. Until they become our own – only then do we become curious as to what all the fuss is about.

This week, Round One, is my turn. Two hundred and fifty games is a bloody long time. How long? Long enough for me to still fret all week about the colour of my footy bootlaces.

This is my 15th AFL season. Back when I started, it went without saying that you wore black boots, kept it simple, no fanfare. You knew that if you were to introduce some fluoro or – God forbid – white boots into your repertoire, you'd be told within seconds that 'you'd better get a kick in those'.

Since those early years, it's been an orgy of showboats and wannabe mavericks. White boots are not only in, they are the new black. The boots have become so loud they have effectively drowned out the dwindling number of 'better get a kick in those' kinda blokes.

For this off-season I've been breaking in a new pair of boots, and while they are technically black, they do have some showy elements. For starters, the laces are bright green. The brightest of bright green. I've been meaning to change the laces all summer and just haven't got around to it yet. Round One can sneak up on you.

I was stretching before training this week, in the athlete's meditation pose, and caught Coach McCartney's eye. He looked at me, and then looked down at my boots. Then he looked away. I've got to get some new laces.

New laces, a new season and new beginnings. The new football year is finally upon us, and after last week's taster, everyone seems ready for the slog of another season. Abraham Lincoln once said, 'If you gave me six hours to cut down a tree I would spend the first four hours sharpening my axe.' This gem could be used for all manner of things in life, but it's particularly pertinent at this time of year.

Pre-seasons are long and arduous. All 18 clubs spend the summer months sharpening their respective axes in anticipation, hoping that when the games begin there are plenty of opposition trees to chop down.

I've had a few people tell me recently that there's a good feeling about the Bulldogs. They're curious about our expectations. 'How much have you improved?' they ask. 'Was the second half of last year a sign of bigger and better things to come?'

I feel people's disappointment when I let their questions hang in the air and float away. I'm not trying to be evasive, it's just that after so long in the caper, I know how hard this competition is. Nothing is banked, nothing is certain.

In 2011 the Western Bulldogs' ship ran aground. When

you go from premiership window to the lower reaches of the ladder, lose your coach and a big handful of senior players, it does feel like your warship has been moored on a sandbar. It's been close to two and a half years since those days, and with a fully embraced vision from our new senior coach, Brendan McCartney, we're all working to drag this big boat back out to sea.

It's been hard work. There have been times out on the field when a few doubts have crept in about our ability, but to a man we've kept our heads down and put our hearts and souls into pushing this lump of steel out of the sand. I look at the second half of last year as the gurgle sound. When our hull finally detached from its sandbar, a tiny piece of forward momentum was earned after 18 months of pushing.

I think we've improved on last year, but talk is cheap. Fremantle have already shown us that they're better, and that's a scary thought. We still need everyone in our colours of red, white and blue to fight, scrap and push the boat to the sunshine of the northern seas. It starts with a tall tree in the country's west, and our job is to cut it down.

A milestone is cause for reflection. Asking a footballer what his club means to him after 250 games is like asking someone what their right arm means to them. It's a part of you and you are a part of it. I don't differentiate the two.

I can't wait to run out onto the most hostile of grounds this Sunday. Who knows what will happen? You hear it all the time: 'We can only control what we can control.' For me, that will start with some new black laces.

20 March 2014

RICKY AND THE ROLL OF THE DICE

Every so often at the Kennel we enjoy an activity that is part Roman empire, part jail riot. We know it as 'The Dice', which has evolved to become 'Ricky Dyson', and is now simply 'Ricky'.

A few years ago someone introduced 'Ricky' as a way of policing minor disciplinary infractions (such as leaving your towel on the floor); it raises a few bucks for a trip away at the end of the year, and lifts morale. We do it every few weeks, but it's greatest impact is usually after a loss.

It's a players-only affair. There is a Boss, who reads out the charges and keeps a record of who's paid his fine and who hasn't. The Boss is overseen by the Grand Poobah, who is generally the oldest player in the room. His call is final when a verdict of guilt or innocence is needed. Here's a garden variety example of what takes place behind closed doors.

Players gather in the theatre, with the Boss standing out front holding the custom-made dice, which is roughly the size of a small television set from the 1980s. A charge will be read out, and the mob will undoubtedly hoot and holler. A chant of 'Ricky, Ricky!' can be heard for miles.

The accused is given a chance to plead his innocence to the Boss, who can hand it over to the Grand Poobah for a potential pardon. In all my time at the Dice, no one has ever been given a pardon.

Once guilt is established, the convicted party is asked to roll the mega-dice in front of the bloodthirsty crowd. When it comes to the actual roll of the dice, the mob is very particular. We like a high toss with plenty of spin. A poor roll – or a 'disrespectful roll' – can result in a 'double roll'. The mob will undoubtedly be in a frenzy from the start, eager to ping someone for a double roll and draw out the anticipation a little longer.

Once 'Ricky' has been successfully rolled and landed on a number from one to six, all eyes turn to the Boss, who has each potential punishment documented in his notes. These penalties can change from year to year and from Boss to Boss.

My personal favourite is the tablespoon of cinnamon in one go. There's a brutality in its simplicity; as Jerry Seinfeld once said, 'Cinnamon enhances everything.'

While this may all sound barbaric to the uninitiated, it is performed in a safe environment and no one is forced to do anything he doesn't want to do. The unwilling can buy their way out with a cash donation, but this is seen as a small price to pay for someone who really would rather not sing a song in front of their teammates.

As a hardened veteran of the mob, I can say there is one thing we really covet: a six. If you happen to roll a six, the room turns into a casino.

Tough decisions now have to be made. With a six on the floor you have the option to cut your losses and pay your way out, or risk it all – double or nothing – on a single roll. Somewhere in the evolution of 'Ricky' this scenario was deemed 'risky', which soon after evolved into 'Rischitelli'. If you roll a six, the primal scream of 'Rischitelli!' will engulf the room.

At this stage, if you roll a two, four or six you have to pay twice. If you roll a one, three or five you are home free.

'Ricky' is silliness turned up to ten. Like the cinnamon, its beauty is in its simplicity. This week we enjoyed our first 'Ricky' session of the year, and it didn't disappoint. The young players continue to plead their innocence, to the disgust of the Grand Poobah, although one pup accepted guilt and the accompanying penalty for straightening his hair at his girlfriend's request. With his hair back to its more familiar curl, he accepted the donation over the 'tell us a joke and make us laugh' option.

After a couple of tough losses and with a big game on the horizon, it doesn't hurt to blow off a little steam. In a recovery sense, 'Ricky' is the equivalent of ten ice baths.

One question is left hanging, though. How will the mob feel about 'Ricky' getting a write up in *The Age*? That's gotta be worth at least one roll, I'd reckon.

3 April 2014

As it turned out, the mob weren't happy when they read this article in The Age. *I had to roll the dice, but only once (I was given some leniency for my good record). I rolled a two, which equated to five slaps on the backside from five different teammates. The mob were delighted at getting their pound of flesh. I, on the other hand, will never be the same.*

OVERT OR SILENT, COURAGE COMES IN MANY FORMS

When I was 18, in one of my first training sessions at Footscray, I led out in a simple lanework drill and the ball hit my hand awkwardly, jarring my finger. I dropped it, grimaced and probably swore before moping to the back of the line to lick my wounds.

There, I heard Tony Liberatore snarl under his breath, 'You've got nine more!'

It was the sort of comment that falls in your mind like a seed in the dirt. Over time, and with the help of a few earthy elements, it begins to grow. I still think about it, even now as a 31-year-old, when I hurt myself during training or a game. Not the exact quote, perhaps, but the spirit of where it came from. Toughen up, get on with the job.

You can't get comfortable playing in the AFL, and last week showed me that again. The game against the Tigers was pretty intense; we were striving for our first win of the year, and they are a serious team who gave us two thumpings last year. To win, we needed all hands on deck, a contribution from everyone. If we had a couple go missing, we would probably lose. That's how it is for a team coming from 15th on the ladder.

At some stage early in the game, our big full-back, Jordan Roughead, went down and looked sore. I didn't see him get hurt, but I thought I could see him holding his stomach in pain. I also know that Roughy is as tough as they come, so if he was staying down, he would have a good reason.

The ball was still in our defensive area and we were on high alert, so despite his ailment, I told him bluntly, 'I need you for a couple of minutes, Rough.'

One of the hard things about footy is that there is barely a stop in play, no timeouts. You have to organise each other on the fly. Messages between teammates tend to be swift, direct and sometimes harsh.

As the afternoon went on and the game ebbed and flowed, I could sense that my big teammate was having a pretty tough day. At one of the breaks he was behind me vomiting, or at least trying to vomit. 'Must've been a nasty one in the guts,' I thought to myself, with all the empathy of a snarling Liberatore. 'He'll be right,' was my next thought.

The second half of the game was dramatic, as is often the way when the Tigers and the Dogs cross paths. We had got out to a lead, but through the sheer will of Trent Cotchin and co., the Tigers were steaming home; the Bulldogs' defence had the air-raid siren sounding loud.

During the chaos, I became aware that Roughy had a sore shoulder. There was no big announcement, I could just tell. Roughy has played with a sore shoulder before, and I casually assumed it was more of the same.

Deep in the third quarter, after he was able to provide another contest in the air and bring the ball to ground, the ball skewed in his direction and he fumbled it twice, almost ending in disaster for the Dogs.

This time I was not so casual. 'We need 40 minutes out of you, Roughy – give me everything you've got. Slap your hands, do whatever you have to do to wake them up!'

Later, Roughy and I were in the showers, his shoulder broken and swollen. I felt foolish and immensely proud in that moment, a most curious combination of emotions. Speaking softly out the corner of a crooked smile, I asked my heroic mate: 'So slapping your hands to wake them up didn't quite help?'

'Not with a snapped AC joint, Bob,' came the reply.

He played almost the whole game with one arm and through immense pain, all for the cause. I didn't hear him complain once. We love him so.

A few days later, as I sat at home with soft rain falling outside, news came through that Mitch Clark would retire from football immediately due to mental health issues. I don't know Mitch Clark or the private challenges he faces, but when I think of him now, walking away from the game at the age of 26 for the betterment of his health, I feel a strange admiration. What I do know is that professional football carries a very unique kind of anxiety and pressure. It's a pressure that is constant, a pressure that is both intensely public and intensely private.

Courage comes in many and varying forms. This week, I saw a couple of them.

10 April 2014

GETTING BEHIND THE UMPIRES IS THE RIGHT DECISION

'The referee is going to be the most important person in the ring tonight besides the fighters.'

GEORGE FOREMAN

About an hour before every game of AFL footy, the three field umpires of the day wander into the changerooms of both teams and shake every player's hand. It's a quaint tradition in a place and time where quaint traditions are on the decline.

Loyal readers will understand my fondness for such a ritual, but I sometimes wonder if we have failed to build on that relationship between players and umpires in the modern era. I often think back to an almost mythical football time where both teams and umpires might gather in a pub or social club after the final siren to talk about the day's play over a glass or two. As my vinyl record collection suggests, I do tend to live in the past.

Footy umpires get a hard time – too hard, for the most part. I sympathise with them because I used to be one.

My wife scoffs when I tell people my very first job was as a field umpire in the Warragul and District Junior Football League. 'You've never worked!' she says. She might have a point.

My time with the whistle was brief (just one season) and

I probably would have done it for free. I got paid – $12.50 a game – and most weekends I did two, the under-12s and the under-14s. Twenty-five dollars a week was a lot of money to me back in 1997; a bag of mixed lollies was my biggest outgoing.

This week marks the Community Umpiring Round in the AFL, and as a former member of the umpiring workforce, I thought I might share a few memories of my time out in the middle in the all-white uniform.

Winters in the Warragul area can be bitterly cold, and I remember that 1997 season being a brutal one. Because the under-12s started at 8.45 am, I'd have to drag my poor old dad out of bed pretty early to make it out to Buln Buln, Hallora, Neerim South or wherever I'd been sent that week. Dad never seemed to mind; he's a kind and patient man, my father.

One of my schoolmates, Brad Nott, was my co-umpire, and we'd go into each team's rooms before the game to meet the coaches and the players and pretend to be adults. I found myself mimicking what I remember our own junior football umpires doing before games. The best example of this was when we would ask the young players to lift their boots for us to run our hands over the studs. Looking for what, I was never quite sure, but I'd seen umpiring stalwarts Mick Rooney and Norm Dorling do it for years.

It wouldn't have mattered if a kid had strapped a razor blade to his boot, because my hands were that numb from the cold I couldn't feel a thing. And besides, most of the kids were about eight years old and more intent on throwing mud at each other than they were about hurting the opposition. Still, every week we'd line these kids up with military precision and scrape their boots with blue, icy hands.

Umpiring the under-12s was more like herding sheep than it was about keeping an eye on taggers and paying free kicks for holding jumpers behind the play. I wish I had a dollar for every time I yelled, 'Play on! Knock it out! Keep it moving!' I'd have made a lot more than $25.

I do look back on those mornings fondly, and the experience did give me a different view of the game that was about to consume my life. Umpiring any game is a tough gig, but I think umpiring a game of AFL football would just about be the toughest.

My first tentative steps as a professional footballer were taken at the Western Bulldogs' affiliate, the Werribee Tigers, in 2000. During one of those early games I watched on as my teammate Andrew Wills took up the debate with our field umpire, and I decided to join in. The umpire turned to me sharply and said, 'Rob, I'll listen to Andrew because he's played 100 games of league footy. You haven't played any. Stay out of it!' It was a great lesson about respect that I never forgot.

Some 15 years later, the Dogs were playing the plucky newcomers of the competition, GWS, in Canberra. The Giants' resident pest, Jacob Townsend, was trying to ruffle my feathers with a miscellaneous repertoire of scallywag tactics when the umpire of the day came over and told the youngster to 'show some respect – he's a veteran of the game'. This only served to increase Townsend's output, but I appreciated the thought. Footy has a funny way of coming full circle.

For anyone going to the football this week, at any level, raise a glass to the umps. Footy needs them.

1 May 2014

AGE-OLD BATTLE
NEVER SEEMS TO PALL

'Getting older is a struggle. I always feel that just under the surface of acceptance and enjoyment of the ageing process is a terrible hysteria just waiting to burst out.'

MICHAEL SHEEN

The ball spills out sideways and I get that sinking feeling. My man has got a step on me and space to move. The ball sits out in front of him and he canters forward to meet it.

This is the lot of a backman – try as you might to stop your opponent from getting an easy kick, inevitably this happens sometimes. It stings every time. In an instant you regroup your thoughts, take stock of what's happening and how you can limit the damage.

On Saturday night at the MCG, against the Demons, I was standing the mark about 40 metres out from goal and the ball was in the hands of Jay Kennedy-Harris, my opponent. He seems a confident young kid – confident with the ball, anyway. I've been watching video of his games all week.

We're close to the boundary, really close. I can hear the voices of the Demons fans over the fence, taunting me. 'He got you there, Murphy . . . He's all over you, Murphy.' I've heard it all before.

I also notice that Kennedy-Harris isn't looking to pass it off, he's going to have a shot. He's confident. My offering of, 'Gee, you're hungry – you haven't even looked to pass the ball!' is at the more generic end of the sledging spectrum. I stopped short of asking him if there was chewy on his boot.

Kennedy-Harris approaches and hits it sweet. I turn to look up at its trajectory, and it's hard not to marvel just a tiny bit at its perfect spin in the perfect setting of the MCG under lights. Fair play to the kid. The crowd erupts and so does Kennedy-Harris.

He's either so happy with the kick that he wants the moment to last a bit longer, or he's so outraged for being thought of as hungry. Either way, he's in my face and letting me know about it. I give him my best 'what are you on about?' look, and the oldest argument in footy rumbles to life. It is the right of every young footballer to take it up to the old blokes on the field with variations of 'you're too old, you're finished'. Just as it is every veteran's right to return fire with a disgusted look and simple query: 'Who are you and what have you done?'

On Saturday night we danced the ancient dance of old and young. Kennedy-Harris was supported by teammate James 'Chip' Frawley, who chimed in with, 'He's only played eight games and he's leading you on a merry dance,' or words to that effect. I was still working on my 'what are you on about?' face, and hit back with, 'That's right, he's only played eight games, and one kick is hardly a reason to break out the champagne.'

Around and around we went. At some point during this exchange I couldn't help but think back to another time when it was me in Kennedy-Harris's shoes. In my very first pre-season at Footscray we were on the back end of a torturous summer and were entering the practice match phase. Two sides were picked, and as we jogged out to our positions I noticed our team's best player (and future hall of famer) Brad Johnson was trotting down towards full-forward.

I was drifting over to my post on the opposition flank and decided to niggle a club icon. 'Are you a forward pocket like Kevin Bartlett now?' I shot at Johnno.

I hang my head in shame now when I think about it. At the time it was a bit of a throwaway line, a kid being a bit cheeky. As the scratch match started moments later, I didn't have time to gauge how my comment was received. It turns out it was received poorly by the smiling assassin.

A few minutes later I found myself waiting under a loopy handball and I sensed trouble in the air. As I took the ball, I turned and something flashed past me. It was Brad Johnson. To avoid being broken into a hundred pieces I must have hit the deck at the last second. As I lay on the wing of the Whitten Oval I had enough awareness to know that Brad must not have been happy with my remark.

It still comes up occasionally when we see each other. He's not as angry about it these days. I don't know what I was thinking, saying that to him before I'd played even one game. And then, on the other hand, I think it's great. Young pups niggling and pushing old dogs to get a growl out of them. You want to see if you're up to it, and if the old dog has any fight left.

The brash confidence of youth and the weathered sentimentality of the aged are destined to conflict on the footy field. It's part of what makes footy interesting.

15 May 2014

LIFE IN THE DOGHOUSE

*'That's it, Murphy, keep chasing. All you've
done today is f—ing chase people!'*
BULLDOGS SUPPORTER, 2001

My dear old ma was outraged when she first heard this being
yelled out to me in the early days of my footy career. Luckily,
my older brother was on hand to give some calming advice:
'It's going to get a lot worse than that, Mum.' He was spot-on.
It got a lot worse.

It's funny, but when you get to talking footy with people
in the park or at a coffee shop, they often feel obliged to bring
you down a peg. 'What about your kicking the other night?'
'Gee, ya miss a lot of left-hand handballs, don't you?'

They don't mean any offence by it, but I get the feeling
some people think we footballers live in ivory towers, kept
away from the criticisms of regular folk. The truth is that our
world is filled with criticism.

Some of it is very public. Opposition supporters and even
some of your own are always on hand when things go awry.
Newspapers and television stations feast on the vulnerable,
and the murky waters of social media trickle constantly under

the surface like bore water. In that sense, the Bulldogs are centre stage at the moment.

That's the public side of things. Inside every club in the AFL there is constant judgement. I sometimes think preparing yourself to play AFL footy is like boarding a fishing boat with 11 holes in it, and you've only got your ten fingers. You have so many things to work on, and often there isn't enough time to get to it all.

You need to be aerobically capable, fast enough, have skills of hand and foot, physical courage and the mental endurance to take in every set play and still play with the freedom of your ten-year-old self when the game restarts. It stretches you to your uppermost limits.

I always think the kids who come into our club with a bit of overconfidence will probably be okay. That bedrock of confidence will be chipped away by a thousand little comments and a few hundred video review sessions. You don't have to go too far in footy to have someone clip you.

I remember a game against Hawthorn early in my career when the ball rolled towards me and at the last moment I looked up to see what was coming at me. I flinched and fumbled the ball. I didn't sleep very well for the next two nights, waiting for it to come up in the review in front of my teammates. I'd let them down.

I got to the club the following Monday, and with sweaty palms sat down in front of Terry Wallace and the other coaches. Then Terry announced there would be no video review that week. My heart leapt.

It's normal to feel uneasy about a video review early in your career. Over time, you begin to look forward to them. They can be cathartic, even if there is a bit of pain or embarrassment to be endured.

This week's review was robust – there was blood on the tracks. Most of us took at least one punch, and when it came to my turn I couldn't help shifting in my seat. I sat watching myself, willing myself to move. *Go now! Push up the ground and stop the flow of play!* But it was too late. I watched myself run backwards, and my team pay a price for that wrong decision.

Ultimately, all these little moments of pain and embarrassment are designed to make you better. Over many years you become hard-wired to judge yourself just as harshly as anyone watching at the ground. The trick is to play with freedom and positivity despite the missteps. It's easier said than done.

Some of my most treasured time in football has been at the top. Winning big games, finals, huge crowds. Strangely enough, some other times that are just as treasured have been while we're languishing at the other end. Beaten, bruised and abandoned. That's when you know you're really part of a club, because after trying so many different ideas to develop a gang mentality, you suddenly find yourselves a tightly bound group of human beings who genuinely feel like it's you against the world.

Of course you'd like more time at the top – who wouldn't? And you don't want to keep returning to the dark shadows we again find ourselves in. But here we are. It's us against the world again.

12 June 2014

BULLDOGS BATTLER LAYS HIS CAREER, AND BODY, TO REST

'Life is not always a matter of holding good cards,
but sometimes playing a poor hand well.'
JACK LONDON

For a time in my life, all footy players smelt like bubblegum. When I was a kid, a packet of footy cards always included a piece of cheap, jaw-breaking pink gum, the smell of which lasted for years. My footy cards were precious to me and I spent hours studying them.

Being from the country meant my access to AFL players was very limited. At our 1991 school fete, Craig Starcevich set up a handball competition. I just stood back and stared, not sure if he was real. Sometimes my dad would take us to Waverley Park to watch a game, but for the most part my connection with the AFL was watching games or highlights of games at home on the television.

Footy players were superheroes to me. They were from another place, and I would watch the marks they took and the goals they kicked in awe and wonder. They inspired me – in the truest sense of the word.

It's hard to keep that sense of wonder as you get older and

the smell of bubblegum fades. The thrill of witnessing a high pack mark is something that never leaves you, but I've found that the things that inspire me have changed a bit since that school fete.

This game is brutal, both on the body and on the heart. In that regard, no one has walked a more painful football path in my time at the Bulldogs than Tom Williams. The pain he has put his body through has been immense; at times, the anguish in his heart has been hard to watch.

Playing at the highest level, time moves so fast. The constant pressure leaves little time to take pause, but this week my teammates and I stopped a while to sit and listen to one of our own tell us he could go no further. Just like a funeral, these times inside a football club are very emotional, and you can't help but reflect on football – and on life.

Through countless operations on his feet and shoulders and dozens of cruel muscle tears, Tom had hardened himself emotionally, always keeping most of the pain to himself. When the time finally came to tell his club he would retire, the walls came down and the tears flowed out of him like a tide.

One of the things that Tom said had poignancy in its simplicity – 'I'm going to miss coming in to this place every day' – and sparked another wave of tears for our mate.

They say every Shakespeare play has a joker, and Tom was ours. He composed himself long enough to specifically thank the teammates who had been with him for the whole journey, but also singled out first-year player Mitch Honeychurch, who, he claimed, 'helped embezzle $3000 through our World Cup draw'. Each of his 85 games may have been hard work, but Tom always got easy laughs.

When a player gets to the end of his career, I imagine he asks himself two things. 'Am I fulfilled?' Only Tom could answer that. The other question is: 'What did I leave behind?' Tom leaves a big chunk of his soul at our club. Like Daniel Menzel at Geelong, when players endure such a wretched run of bad luck through injury, their resilience to keep at it puts them in the hearts of everyone they play with.

Every effort to crawl your way out of the darkness and back onto the field takes a toll. Each lap of the swimming pool may have felt like a wasted, lonely journey, but the courage to keep going inspires those around them. Tom inspired me.

A few weeks ago, *The Age*'s Peter Hanlon asked me to sum up Tom in a word, but I couldn't think of one that captures the happy, manic, complicated man. I tried this week, but instead asked myself, 'If I close my eyes and think of Tom, what do I see?' I see Tom laughing.

And after all he's been through, I think that says a bit.

10 July 2014

A CHANGING OF THE GUARD OUT WEST

Our club theme song sounded different this week. It sounded louder and came from deeper in our bellies.

You don't get blasé about winning games of footy in the AFL – at least, I don't. They've been all too rare. But I have to admit that when we started up our tribal hymn in Cairns with a ferocious 'Dada-deda-da-DA . . . Sons of the WEST', it rocked me back on my heels. This one really meant something to our group.

There were so many young faces who ran out onto Cazaly's Stadium on Saturday night for the red, white and blue, but none of them seemed overawed. It's one thing to play young guys, give them a chance and see if they can cut it. It's another thing to take careful time to find out which ones can do it, and who will take a club forward.

I see in this crop of Bulldog youngsters a strong self-belief. It's a privileged position I have, watching them grow on the field. Sometimes the winds of change are so subtle you barely feel it. At other times they whip you across the face like the salty sea of the Bass Strait.

From the moment the final siren sounded in Cairns, something felt different. The song roared and then we adjourned to our changerooms to spend a few minutes together, taking off strapping and patting each other on the back. The simple joy of the victors.

Every sporting team has an internal energy source. For a long time, I have been very much at the coalface of that. On Saturday night I felt the soft winds of change across my face. The internal source of energy within our team is changing. In the best possible sense, this is not my team any more. I still have an important role to play, but out on the ground on the weekend I went along for the ride, while the burning fires of propulsion came from a new generation of Footscray's finest.

If this litter of pups can push themselves and each other on to bigger and better things, I think the win on Saturday night might be seen as a pivotal step on that path. There'll be some missteps along the way, for we aren't in calm seas yet. But I trust what I heard in the song. Good young lads, all of them.

As is often the way, in football and in life, one moment you're pausing to look at the fresh new faces who have it all in front of them, and the next you're tipping your hat to another who has decided that this year will be his last. Lenny Hayes has been the player you wanted to be, wanted to have and the player you'll never forget.

I once wrote a column on mateship in footy and the truism that, win or lose, one of the great things about the game is who you get to play alongside. Typical of the times we live in, my self-esteem rested purely on how many people retweeted it. My phone alerted me at one point that Hayes had retweeted me. It was like Elvis Presley dedicating 'Blue Suede Shoes' to me at a Vegas show. Hmmm, the power of Lenny.

I don't know anything about the inner workings of the St Kilda Football Club, but if I had to bet on who was the energy source in the changerooms, I would put my last dollar on Lenny Hayes being the man. Every time we played against the Saints, and there were a few big matches, he always found a way to impose himself on the game.

His tackle on Easton Wood a couple of years ago is something I've kept coming back to this week. Sometimes a single act can have a huge impact on a game, just like a single player or a cluster of players can have a huge impact on a club.

For the Bulldogs, I hope this next cluster can take the torch and run with it. For Lenny Hayes, all anyone can do is raise a glass to a footballer who's been one of the finest of all.

17 July 2014

LIFE: SLAM DUNK OR BASKET CASE?

'He used to let me win.' I'll never forget the moment when I realised my dad was throwing games of tennis.

A couple of years ago I was reminiscing about some epic tennis matches we used to have on the courts just opposite my primary school. I was thinking to myself that I must've been a pretty good little player to beat my dad, who was a versatile and accomplished sportsman.

Then I had a flash of memory, a foggy image of launching the ball from the service line. In an instant the bubble burst. Suddenly I saw things much clearer. 'He used to let me win.'

When I was a kid I just assumed that when I was fully grown I would be able to dunk the basketball. I stopped playing the sport competitively when I was about 14 or 15, so it's only in recent months that I've come to realise the unfortunate truth. I can't dunk. I won't dunk. I will never dunk.

That's one of the hard things about growing up that I'm starting to see all too often: life isn't a matter of crossing off a never-ending list of accomplishments, it's more a case of watching on helplessly as yet another thing is added to the list of things you'll never do.

I was never much of a shooter, but when I missed two lay-ups in a row in front of my teammates recently, I took it pretty hard. To break up the monotonous routine that a football season can become, the coaches had decided to set up a basketball-themed warm-up before our recovery skills session out on the cold and windy Whitten Oval a few weeks ago. Most of the young blokes at our footy club fancy themselves as basketballers; a few of them dress like NBA players too.

When I told them that I used to be pretty handy as a kid playing for the Warragul Gladiators, they didn't pay me much attention. To be frank, I was dismissed as a silly old man talking about his heyday. As the warm-up drills started on the court, the ball came my way and within a minute I'd missed twice. I loped up to the basket, caressed the ball onto the backboard . . . and missed. By a long way.

I got that awful twinge. Am I past it?

I was still thinking about the missed shots a few days later, the memories tugging at my thoughts. It didn't help that Lin Jong and a few others kept reminding me about my clunky shooting every time I passed them at the Kennel.

This traumatic event has forced me into action. As a way for my wife and three children to spend some quality time together, we're all working on our jump shots. On most afternoons you'll find the Murphys up at the local primary school throwing skyhooks and bucket shots.

The first few practice sessions were pretty diabolical. I couldn't make a basket, and each time I shot the ball it felt different to the last. I had no rhythm, an uncomfortable state that was made even more acute by the fact that every time our little four-year-old, Frankie, got the ball, she headed for the playground. I don't know what sport she thinks we're playing.

Justine is the best shooter in our family. She has this uncanny knack of scoring points when no one is watching. Six-year-old Jarvis is tall and might one day become a fine basketball player – if he picks up the ball instead of climbing trees. And Delilah (six months old), it has to be said, is poor on defence. To anyone passing by, we must look a sight. This week's practice sessions have seen improvement in all of us. Is there a sweeter sound in sport than 'swish'?

In the AFL, the twinge of Father Time is felt all through the 18 clubs at this time of year. So many great players have called time on their careers in just the past few weeks, and there would be plenty still who will be tussling with the toughest question of all for a footballer to answer: 'Am I past it?'

After mulling it over myself in recent months, I was very excited and grateful to sign on for another year at my football club. Fifteen years down this old road and I still like the scenery. Who knows when it will end?

At our family shootout last night, I decided to give it one more go. I wanted to try for a slam dunk. With my family of cheerleaders there to witness it, I dribbled, ran and launched for the basket. SLAM DUNK!

It was a moment of pure exhilaration, one I really hammered up for the kids. Always the voice of reason, Justine pointed out in a whisper, 'That basketball ring isn't regulation height, you know ...'

'It doesn't matter,' I shot back. 'It'll be years before the kids know the truth about their slam-dunking dad.'

My dad let me win, and I love that about him. Perhaps my three will be just as understanding.

24 July 2014

THE BLOKES
I LOVE TO PLAY

The trip down to Launceston is one I look forward to every year. Such a calm and pretty town.

I woke early on Sunday morning and snuck out the door, careful not to wake my new roommate, Dale Morris, and went in search of a coffee. Armed with little more than my warmest clothes, a beanie and my book, *Jasper Jones*, I walked the foggy downtown streets for close to an hour. There was barely another soul around.

It seemed there were cosy-looking pubs on every corner, and all around me tree-lined streets that snaked their way up steep hills. It's my kind of town. If only things were as serene out on York Park.

It's hard to imagine the Hawks not being a part of this year's Grand Final. Like all great teams, they seem to move as one, whether they have the ball or are trying to get it off you. We battled hard for most of the game, but when the Hawks tightened their grip, it felt hard to breathe.

They say a champion team will always defeat a team of champions, but as a kid I was obsessed with writing up teams, footy teams of my own creation that could beat anyone. Having just witnessed a few of my favourite players up close at the weekend, I thought it might be interesting to pen my favourite team of AFL players.

When I did this as a kid, my team was full of Richmond players, but I'm an adult now so I won't put any Bulldogs players in – not even Marcus Bontempelli – because it's not cool to brag about your kids.

The criteria is flimsy and whimsical. They are my favourites. Today. Tomorrow, they could all be gone. So, in the spirit of a ten-year-old scrawling his backline, midfield, forwards and followers, here they are, Bob's 22.

BACKS

Jeremy Howe, Melbourne: Master of the most beautiful part of the game. Saves his best for the Dogs, so I get good seats.

Ted Richards, Sydney: Told half a story at a Players' Association conference once and couldn't remember the other half. Good player, too.

Luke Hodge, Hawthorn: Direction and voice is like a 19th man. Playing near him made me better.

HALF-BACKS

Pearce Hanley, Brisbane / Zach Tuohy, Carlton: I wanted both because they're good, and Irish. Forced to choose, I'd pick Tuohy because his dad worked in a prison.

Harry Taylor, Geelong: Told me while shaking my hand after a game that he read the column. Flattery gets you in.

Tendai Mzungu, Fremantle: File under one of those players who's really hard to play on and doesn't get the credit he deserves.

CENTRE

Nat Fyfe, Fremantle: Almost excluded because it's so obvious. Beautifully balanced, can do it all on the field, best head of hair since Brett Kirk. In a two-team town, his life must be hell.

Lenny Hayes, St Kilda: Can you imagine a team of favourites without him?

Callan Ward, GWS: The toughest and vaguest footballer I've ever seen.

HALF-FORWARDS

Luke Breust, Hawthorn: He's the one who started the list after two senior teammates nominated him their favourite.

Matthew Pavlich, Fremantle: Class captain of my '99 draft.

Jack Gunston, Hawthorn: Classic footballer – lean, tall, leads hard, marks well, kicks straight.

FORWARDS

Mark LeCras, West Coast: Liam Picken and I double-teamed him one day; we kept him to a couple and felt like we'd held Coleman. A gun.

Jarryd Roughead, Hawthorn: Just shaded Tex Walker, but had to be here: Lenny's heir apparent as the game's favourite player.

Steve Johnson, Geelong: Inspired my most popular column – about getting beaten by Stevie J.

FOLLOWERS

Aaron Sandilands, Fremantle: He's like one of the wonders of the world – you've just gotta go and have a look at him up close.

Tom Rockliff, Brisbane: Once told me on the ground he'd been having coffee with my wife. Ben Hudson was nearby, laughing.

Jordan Lewis, Hawthorn: The one opponent I know I'll see every week. Might even be a better bloke than Brad Sewell.

INTERCHANGE

Ben Hudson, Adelaide, Brisbane, Bulldogs, Collingwood: Making this team puts him level with Dale Kickett as the game's greatest journeyman.

Ryan Crowley, Fremantle: I've always wanted to have a tagger I can unleash.

Ryan O'Keefe, Sydney: Can't get a game for the Swans but he can for me. Showed me how hard a flanker can run.

Dayne Zorko, Brisbane: Had to fill our Dayne quota. Nice alphabetical finish. Can play, too.

7 August 2014

---

*That weekend my Bulldogs were playing St Kilda, and a
certain blond centre half-forward, with a crooked smile, wondered
aloud how on earth he hadn't made this 22.*

THE LAST WALTZ

'If I miss anything about the sport, it's the camaraderie of old teammates.'
BO JACKSON

Before every game, I'll make my way over to meet him. He's expecting me. We'll pick up a couple of footies and the routine begins. Our waltzing ritual. No matter how nervous I am or how unfamiliar the place we're playing, once we start up I feel like I'm home.

I don't know when we started this routine, but we've been doing it a long time, 12 years or so, and I always go first. Gia starts throwing both footies at me, one after the other, and I get them back to him as best I can with short, quick handballs.

After a little while he'll start the countdown from 30 all the way back to one. We take a couple of steps back to give ourselves a bit more room and he'll start kicking the ball into my hands. I wait until I've marked it 13 times; it's a tip of the hat to my best mate who carries this number on his back, although I've never told him that.

From there, we lengthen out and I lead at his stab passes, slowly retreating and surging again. After that I make a shorter lead, but this time the ball is rolled at my feet and I have to get low, watch for the bounce and take it cleanly in my hands. Once I've done half a dozen or so, I stand up straight to finish with ten more kicks in the hands.

Then we swap. I become the thrower, kicker and roller. It's just a warm-up, and a simple one at that, but perhaps because we've been doing it for so long, it's become something else, something far more special.

There've been many times this season when I've got to thinking about our time in footy together. He's been my great mate through it all, but it's only this week that I've come to see our little warm-up as a metaphor for what he's given me. More than anyone else, Danny has taught me the importance of routine, of work ethic and attention to detail. He's taught me how much it takes to play this game against the best. He's taught a few others along the way too.

In the beginning we weren't that fond of each other. Both of us arrived at Footscray on the same day, and we watched from the old social club as the players started their pre-season time trials out on the Whitten Oval. We never had a falling out and no cross words were exchanged, but for the first half of our debut season we just didn't click. In some ways, we are very different.

Thinking about my mate this week, I wondered if our shaky start had something to do with the fact that we were always pitted against each other. Whether it was on the field or in the gym, our names were always next to each other's, and a competitive streak ran between us like a river on a map. I've never told him this, but there were times when we had testing in the gym that I'd find out how much he'd lifted and, with just a hint of spite, do one more.

I can't say for sure, but there may still be some spite in Danny's gut. Last year I started writing a column that was meant to be my version of Jack Kerouac's *On the Road* – a roaming stream of consciousness about an AFL road trip to Canberra.

As I followed my muse, I flippantly typed the words, 'In all likelihood, this will be the Fossil's last year.' It was not my place to say it, and by the time I realised that, it was in print and too late. Even though he never confronted me about it in any serious way, I think it pissed him off. My bitter work in the gym all those years ago came back to haunt me when, at the end of last season, Danny said, 'I'll do one more.'

He's a determined bastard. To not just survive but thrive at AFL level on a forward flank for 265 games is testament to his skill and courage. He's been a hugely influential person in our football club – far more than most people outside the club would realise, I suspect.

On Sunday, Danny will run out in the red, white and blue for the very last time. I hope we can send him out the right way and make it a joyous celebration in front of our supporters. His wife, Kelly, and his children, Ruby and Otis, will be watching, along with his parents, Joe and Jenny, and his sisters, Rachel and Sara. Family is everything to Danny. This week, when he got up to talk to his teammates about the end of his career and what it all meant, he described us as his 'brothers'.

This time of the year is often emotional for sides that miss the finals. Football clubs inherently have an eye on the future, but this week we pause for a little while to say goodbye. On Sunday one of the hardest parts of the day will come ten minutes before our first warm-up when I wander over to meet my dear mate. Where once, for a short time, there was an embarrassing slither of spite, now there is a belly full of love and admiration for my Bulldog brother. I know he'll be expecting me.

And I'm honoured that we'll get to play together one more time.

28 August 2014

THE ROUTINE
WE ALL WISHED
WOULD CONTINUE

A footy season is built on routine and then more routine. When the season eventually crashes and burns to the ground, as it did for the Bulldogs on Sunday night, it can leave you feeling a little lost. No amount of cold beer or fancy dress can mask the disappointment or fill the emptiness in the hours that follow, but we try anyway.

Following the awfully named 'Mad Monday' is a day sometimes referred to on the inside as 'Terrible Tuesday'. This is the final day of routine in a footballer's season, and if you've had a year like ours, it's not much fun. On this day you bounce from one meeting to the next – it's like speed dating, only there are no potential life partners sitting opposite you, just your bosses.

Your first date is with the medical staff, where your year of ill health is opened up in front of you. For the first time in quite a while, I played every game this year and there won't be any post-season surgery for me. Despite this clean bill of health, it took a good ten or 15 minutes to work through the various bumps and bruises accumulated over a season. There are injuries to hips and A/C joints I can barely even remember. It's been a long year.

Compared to other years, when I've been on crutches already or sent straight to hospital for surgery, this year has been a success – in a medical sense at least. I thank my group of 'Weary' Dunlops, we shake on it and hope for more of the same next year.

Next up is the big daddy of blind dates, your individual coaches' review – and there are about nine of them in there! I'm not nervous about going in until I'm in there, when all of a sudden I've got all nine bosses sitting there looking at me. The palms start to sweat and my mouth feels as dry as a biscuit.

It doesn't make sense to be nervous; after 15 years in this job there shouldn't be too many surprises at the end of the year. All season long feedback flows through the corridors of footy clubs like a spring creek.

The nerves must have been embedded in me from long ago, as a young recruit facing a much smaller but still intimidating firing squad of Terry Wallace and his lieutenants. When you start out at AFL level there can be more than a couple of surprises at this time of year which can be difficult to absorb if your hide is not sufficiently hardened.

I remember in my first or second year being sat in front of Plough and listening to his assessment of me while trying to look him straight in the eye. To my horror, he started to shrink before my eyes! The hangover I was sporting obviously wasn't helping, but along with the general stress of the situation it created a cocktail of vertigo.

I tried to listen carefully and keep my eye contact solid, but after the ten-minute dressing-down Plough seemed 25 metres away, when in fact if I reached out I could have touched his nose. No wonder he thought I was a space cadet back then.

Thankfully, the same didn't happen with Macca and the other coaches this year. They all stayed right where they were, and although some scars remain from those early years, I emerged from the meeting with a mixed bag but an overall sentiment similar to that of the medical department. Played every game, not a bad result for everyone.

Walking out of my meeting, I saw a few players in various states of nervous tension, waiting their turn. A couple were pacing up and down the gym. This day takes its pound of flesh.

With the individual evaluations complete, we came together as a group for one last team meeting of the year. This time, there is no strategy, no enemy over the hill. Even the tones of voice sound different, softer, more considered. The war is over for 2014.

Management tie off a few loose ends and there's a quick run-through of the expectations on every player for their time off and the fitness level we'll all need to be at when we return. It's a sobering thought. All that's left after that is to clean out your locker and go home. The routine that's ruled our lives for ten months evaporates, and for a while the empty feelings in my stomach bump and sway.

I'm really looking forward to the first final on Friday night between the Hawks and Cats. It'll be a beauty, these two old foes know no other way. If it goes down to the wire, as I think it will, the empty feeling in my gut may just start to fade a little. That's the power of finals footy.

As much as there's liberation in being let off a footballer's leash, becoming a spectator overnight at this time of year only makes me wish the routine had continued for a while longer.

4 September 2014

CLASSIC BATTLE
ABOUT TO BEGIN

I had a most wonderful human experience last week. I was up at the local basketball court with my family (we're still working on our jump shots) and chatting with the Bowden brothers, Joel and Pat. Joel lives around the corner from me and Pat was visiting from Perth. I've known them for many years; I played with Pat at the Bulldogs in the early part of the 2000s.

As we were shooting the breeze and the odd air ball, a young fella strolled through the park right up to us, and in a slightly fidgety way asked, 'Who wants to play one v one?' We all hesitated, then turned him down; it was almost home time and we had on work boots and dress shoes.

The young lad who laid down the challenge could have been aged anywhere from 14 to 18 – it's hard to tell, isn't it? His name was Henry. As we continued to chat and pretend to chase our kids, Henry kept shooting the ball, all the while gently goading us into a game.

Eventually I cracked. 'All right, Henry, let's play a little.'

The battle began. Under the watchful eye of my amused friends, confused kids and an embarrassed wife, Henry and I went toe to toe. A couple of things became apparent right away: I missed a lot, and Henry talked a lot. The more Henry trash-talked, the more I missed, and the game that was supposed to be decided once someone landed five buckets went on for far too long. (I blamed the work boots.)

Sweating like a pig, I eventually made that fifth basket, but there was no celebratory song. Henry took a moral victory. I think he just wanted to taunt an old man. As he left the court, headed for home, I could still hear him teasing me over his shoulder. I really liked Henry. I think there will be a rematch at some stage.

It's that time of year. One versus one. With my footy season turning to dust a few weeks ago, I've spent that time side-stepping between the AFL and VFL finals series. I didn't think the VFL Grand Final could deliver on the Preliminary Final from the week before at the Borough, but in front of a whopping 24,000 people at Etihad Stadium our Footscray boys swept us into scenes of jubilation in the stands with an inspiring win.

'Development' is the mantra of the VFL sides with direct alignment to an AFL club, and Footscray coach Chris Maple has stayed true to that for the whole year. But when you make it to a Grand Final it's all about winning, and win they did.

There was a great feeling in the rooms after the game. The pure joy and satisfaction on the players' faces left a big impression on me. I was with Matthew Boyd as we left the change-rooms, and on our way back to the car we could see something out on the ground that we were both drawn to. Through a caged fence in the Etihad car park, our view was a little skewed, but we could see and hear the entire VFL team back out in the middle of the ground singing 'Sons of the 'Scray'. That's what it's all about.

Sidestepping back to the AFL, we are down to the final two. Sydney and Hawthorn have been the two best teams all year. Sydney is playing football at the moment that is like a symphony, each player hitting the right note at the right time, but it's Buddy's sheet music they're playing from. What has he written for Saturday, and can the Swans play it so perfectly again?

Hawthorn got the shock of its life last Saturday night against the barnstorming Power. I sat on the couch with my heart beating out of my chest as they lunged for the line against the hardened Hawks. If anyone can topple the Swans it's the reigning premier, but it'll take their best.

It's the classic battle of two. One versus one. Just like Henry said.

At 2.30 this Saturday the question will be asked of both teams, of every player. Who wants to play? Don't expect to see hesitation. They'll go to war. It'll end with one team out on the field, all alone, arm in arm, singing their tribal song. Football heaven.

24 September 2014

ACKNOWLEDGEMENTS

I want to start by thanking the Western Bulldogs Football Club. If there are rivers running through this book, then one of them must be my connection to the Kennel. I could've played nowhere else.

I also want to dip my hat to the crew at Nero Books. Your enthusiasm for the game and for good storytelling has made me feel right at home. Along with Kathryn and Tom from Stride Management, I hope this book is just the start of a larger conversation down the years.

This book would never ever have got off the ground if I hadn't been given the chance to write for *The Age*. I thank the paper for taking a risk on me and letting me roam the hills of my imagination unimpeded.

The generosity of *The Age*'s journalists over the years has also been a great help. I do wish to single out one in particular. Peter Hanlon has been a guiding influence on my pen since the very first column. His tender touch is sprinkled through these pages like tinsel on a Christmas tree. He is one of my heroes, my liniment comrade.

To my sister, Bridget, and her husband, Ben (Souma), and to my brother, Ben, and his wife, Stephanie: I want to thank you for your support, and for all the adventures we had as kids. I think Herbie would have been proud of us.

To Mum and Dad: I think a hug would probably say it best. With a few words, I'd love to be able to put my arms around you both and say thank you. For so many things, but most of all for letting me dream big, and damn the cost.

And to my wife, Justine, and our three children, Jarvis, Frankie and Delilah: I love you more than Melbourne rain, I love you more than Paul Kelly singing about Melbourne rain. How did I get this lucky? Must be the Irish in me . . . *Sláinte*.

Lightning Source UK Ltd.
Milton Keynes UK
UKOW04f1820271015

261485UK00004B/237/P